W9-COZ-120

To Steve, for making it happen

Acknowledgements

Thanks to all who answered my questions: David Goldbeck of Ceres Press, Mark Ortman of Wise Owl Books, and Marty Lee of Gibbs Smith. I especially thank my family—my husband and son for their support, patience and encouragement during this undertaking, and my parents for their loving enthusiasm.

Contents

Beginnings 6
Chapter 1: Basic principles 12
Planning 14
Wedding timeline 20
Chapter 2: Invitations 26
Chapter 3: Choosing a wedding
or reception site 33
Chapter 4: Ceremony 38
Chapter 5: Clothes 40
Personal care 52
Chapter 6: Decorations, flowers 67
Chapter 7: Music, photography, gifts 85
Chapter 8: Food 93
Chapter 9: Odds and ends—
Favors 130
Candles 134
Cleanup 137
Departure 137
Chapter 10: Honeymoon 139
Resources: Selected bibliography
Books 148
Articles 152
Magazines 153
Newsletters 154
Catalogs 155
Appendix: Recycled papermaking 156
Cornstarch clay 156
Index: 160

Beginnings

This book originated when my husband and I were planning our own wedding. We wanted a ceremony and reception that reflected our love of the wilderness and concern for the environment. After searching in vain for books with advice on planning such a wedding, we did our own research instead. We came up with a green wedding that was fun to plan, and truly meaningful to us.

Why have a green wedding in the first place? The answer lies in opportunity. There are all sorts of wonderful ways to celebrate your wedding in a manner that does not literally cost the earth— from recycling and composting, to choosing socially and environmentally responsible vendors for your wedding services, to consuming less. And there are more and more businesses that are catering to the needs and wishes of environmentally conscious consumers, more opportunities for recycling and other earth-friendly practices than ever before.

A 1992 survey by *Bride's & Your New Home* magazine indicates that the "average" wedding costs $15,968, honeymoon not included. And adding honeymoon, engagement, wedding and household furnishings together totals up to a $32 billion industry, according to an estimate by *Bride's* magazine. There is a tremendous potential for making that money do double duty by channeling it to socially and environmentally responsible businesses and causes.

This is not an all-encompassing "green lifestyle" book. Many excellent ones already exist, and are included in the selected bibliography at the back of the book. Rather, this book is a green lifestyle book with a narrow focus—your wedding—that spills into everyday living. It is my hope that as you read of different ways of doing things for your wedding day, that you will want to incorporate some of them into your daily lives.

Many of the ideas in this book come from ways that things were done in the past. I regard this not as a "backward" step, but as a second look at forgotten methods from the past that are less wasteful or toxic.

Unfortunately, books and the information in them go out of date. Companies change locations, phone numbers, their marketing focus, or go out of business altogether. Because of this, I will be publishing a quarterly Green Weddings Newsletter through Paper Crane Press, P.O. Box 29292, Bellingham, WA 98228-1292. Please write to me, in care of Paper Crane Press, with suggestions and news, and to subscribe. This information will also be used in revised editions of this book.

The best way to keep abreast of what is available to you as a consumer is to read a good newspaper.

Much of the information I found was from follow-up I did on articles I read in*The Christian Science Monitor;* some leads were obtained from the local daily paper. You will find that as you research information, facts relevant to your research seem to cross your path all the time.

I wish you much pleasure as you work toward your own wedding celebration. May you enjoy the journey and the destination equally!

What is a green wedding?
A green wedding is earth-sensitive.

Recycling possibilities are constantly increasing. We can recycle newsprint, scrap paper, cardboard, glass, batteries, tin, aluminum, plastics, motor oil, solvents, building materials, appliances, and more. And it is possible to choose products and services from a number of companies that are green in various ways. Some use a more benign manufacturing process, donate a portion of their profits to support the environment, use recycled materials, or purchase raw materials or finished products from indigenous peoples that live in harmony with their environment. A good, yearly updated resource for this kind of information is Co-op America's *National Green Pages,* which is included with other catalogs in the Resources section at the back of this book. It lists all sorts of green businesses and their products, and costs about the same as a paperback novel.

A green wedding is affordable.
When your money is yours, you have control of it and how it is invested. If you have to take out a

bank loan to finance something, the money that you repay the bank is being invested by the bank, not by you. Bank investments are typically not very earth-friendly (see the *National Green Pages* for exceptions). If you spend less and borrow less—or none at all—you have more money to spend in ways that are helpful to the planet, including donations to environmental organizations.

A green wedding cuts down on excess.

Although people in the United States comprise only about seven percent of the world's population, we use one third of the world's resources. One way for us to help correct this imbalance is to cut back on our own consumption.

Voluntary Simplicity by Duane Elgin (William Morrow, rev. ed. 1993) discusses the attractions of living a more frugal lifestyle. A practical resource along the same lines is Randi Hacker's*How to Live Green, Cheap, and Happy: Save Money! Save the Planet!* (Stackpole Books, 1994). *Choose to Reuse* by Nikki and David Goldbeck (Ceres Press, 1995) is a very thorough resource of services, products and programs that promote reuse; it lists over 2,000 resources and more than 200 topics.

A green wedding is healthy, safe, and inclusive.

Unless wine is a part of your ceremony for religious reasons, alcoholic beverages are not "really" necessary. With all the sparkling waters, fruit juices and mineral waters on the market, there is plenty of choice, and often health-conscious people would actually prefer a glass of non-alcoholic sparkling fruit juice to champagne or wine. A non-alcoholic selection of beverages, including one for toasting, is more inclusive, allowing everyone—children, adults with alcohol sensitivities, and those with health problems—to participate fully in the festivities. It also reduces the risk of post-reception traffic accidents. Alcoholic beverages also have empty calories, rob the body of vital nutrients, and are seldom made with organically-grown ingredients. And some wedding locations are closed to a reception with alcohol, eliminating the green option of having the ceremony and reception at the same location.

A green wedding celebrates a carefully considered commitment to marriage.

This kind of long-term thinking is useful for our entire experience, including our relationship to the world in which we live. Short term thinking can be disastrous not only on the environmental level, but on the personal level as well. The wedding ceremony is not more important than the marriage it is supposed to initiate, yet with the emphasis on the material aspects of wedding planning, our society seems to invest more time in planning its weddings than its marriages.

In the context of an article I wrote about people's prenuptial misgivings and subsequent marriages, I interviewed individuals who had serious doubts prior to their weddings. A surprising number admitted that they had decided to go through with the ceremony anyway, because of all the preparations that had been made, and the expense. Those with major concerns had serious problems later on, some insurmountable. It seems that two possible solutions to this problem are more careful thought before the wedding (long-term thought), and less elaborate material preparations (short-term thought).

If the focus of wedding planning is the up-coming commitment, and not attire or reception decor, chances are good that details will not overwhelm the real meaning of the wedding. A good book about marriage and commitment is *Married People: Staying Together in the Age of Divorce,* by Francine Klagsbrun (Bantam Books, 1985).

Most importantly, remember that somewhere between the cake and the kiss, the clothes and the candles, is the celebration of the start of a marriage—yours.

Chapter 1: Basic Principles; Planning; Wedding Timeline

Basic Principles

There are some very simple principles behind planning for a greener wedding—or living daily life, for that matter:

• Avoid disposable and one-time-use items. For weddings, these include women's hosiery with wedding bell appliqués; disposable cameras; plastic and tulle bride-and-groom or wedding bell cake top ornaments; parasols, fans and gloves for female attendants; cheap, tacky wedding favors that guests will only throw away; table decorations that are so specific to your wedding that they cannot be reused or given as gifts. You can probably think of many others.

• Check to see if you can use borrowed, rented, or secondhand items before you purchase new ones.

• If new items are purchased, make sure they are of good quality so that they will have a long and useful "life."

• Ask yourself: Do I/we really need this item? Will its absence detract from the meaning or beauty of the ceremony, of the day? What meaning does it have for me/us? A good book for increasing our awareness of which items have symbolism to us personally is *Rituals for Our*

Times, by Evan Imber-Black, Ph.D., and Janine Roberts, Ed.D. (Harper Collins, 1992).

• Select wedding garb—for yourselves and attendants—that can be worn again, if you don't borrow or rent it.

• Recycle or use products made out of recycled materials. Use as few virgin resources as possible, especially nonrenewable ones.

• Choose products that are available in bulk, or with minimal packaging.

• Avoid all aerosol products, whether for household or personal use.

• Use organically grown food. Not only a health concern, the consumption of organically-grown foodstuffs puts fewer toxic pesticides and fertilizers into the environment and food chain, and promotes sustainable agriculture.

• Consider a vegetarian menu at your reception. Plant proteins (legumes, vegetables, grains, fruits) use fewer valuable resources—less land and water—per pound than livestock.

• Use organically grown, local flowers in season—or grow your own. Locally grown flowers don't need much transportation to get to you. Out of season flowers will have to be transported long distances, contributing to pollution (and costing a small fortune). Leave wildflowers in the wild where they belong, so they can reseed for the future.

• Reduce electricity use—consider the use of candles instead of electric light and live, "unplugged" music at your reception or ceremony.

• Cut down on excess transportation and reduce air pollution at the same time. Arrange your reception at the same location as the wedding, or within easy walking distance. Consider a nearby honeymoon.

• Choose products from companies and countries that do not use child labor.

• Use products of companies that donate a portion of their profits to environmental causes.

Simplify whatever you can, wherever you can, without compromising the meaning that this day will have for you. Fewer small details to attend to will translate into more fun, more time for your guests, less stress and less overconsumption.

Planning

The focus of this book is on how to creatively use products and services in a way that benefits— or at least is less harmful to—the environment. I hope that you will find much useful information here on how to create a joyous occasion that is a reflection of your convictions.

Since this book concentrates on how to invent and/or select green options for your wedding, you won't find in here the type of details such as charts detailing how to seat people for a formal dinner, information on how to write your own vows, or how to find wedding bargains. These types of subjects are already expertly covered in dozens of helpful, informative books which you can check out of the library for free.

So, before buying any books on wedding planning, go to the library and look at what they have in their collection. To see what is currently in print and can be ordered through bookstores, go to the reference section, check the current year's *Books in Print* (R.R. Bowker, publisher) and look under the "wedding" categories in the Subject Guide. Using this method, I was able to find out about several interesting new books that had not yet appeared in my local bookstore. *Whitaker's Books in Print* is a similar reference. After you've done this preliminary research, then you'll have a better idea of what information you want. Excellent books for planning various types of weddings abound. If you buy a new book, choose one that suits as many of your needs as possible. Here are just a few. For all aspects of traditional contemporary wedding planning, see Carroll Stoner's *Weddings for Grownups* (Chronicle Books, 1993). It includes details for everything from wedding budgets to how to conduct business with professionals such as caterers, musicians and florists. *The Everything Wedding Book: Everything You Need to Know to Survive Your Wedding and Actually Even Enjoy It!* by Janet Anastasio and Michelle Bevilaqua (Bob Adams, Inc., 1993), is quite consumption-oriented, but has wedding customs, planning worksheet space, tips on buying rings, degrees of wedding formality and appropriate attire—good if you're planning a large formal wedding. Another good source, with details of couples' experiences and advice, and a chapter devoted to intercultural and interfaith weddings, is *Creative Weddings* by Laurie Levin and Laura Golden Bellotti (Penguin, 1994). If you're getting married in winter around

Christmas, and want to have a Christmas theme for your wedding, or if you just want some good ideas, look at *The New Green Christmas* by the Evergreen Alliance (Halo Books, 1991; see Bibiography for address). For good, solid advice on how to save money during all phases of wedding planning, see *1001 Ways to Save Money...and Still Have a Dazzling Wedding*, by Sharon Naylor (Contemporary Books, 1994). *Tried and Trousseau* by Jennifer Rogers (Fireside/ Simon & Schuster, 1992) is a funny, irreverent book with lots of useful information no one else has. A lovely and practical book that traces the history of Jewish wedding customs and explores their applications today is Anita Diamant's *The New Jewish Wedding* (Summit Books, 1985). *Jumping the Broom: the African-American Wedding Planner* by Harriette Cole (Henry Holt & Co., 1992), is another thoroughly researched resource with some refreshing ideas. For non-traditional ceremonies and a description of wedding customs of many cultures, from Australian to Zulu, a good resource is Richard Leviton's *Weddings By Design* (Harper San Francisco, 1993). *I Do—A Guide to Creating Your Own Unique Wedding Ceremony*, by Syndey Barbara Metrick, (Celestial Arts, 1992), breaks down and analyzes the various components of the ceremony to help you write your own. It is one of the best contemporary ceremony-writing books I have found. Again, for the most recent titles, see *Books in Print*.

Another book with a ceremony-oriented approach to wedding planning is *The Wedding*

Book by Howard Kirschenbaum and Rockwell Stensrud (The Seabury Press, 1974). It also includes the origins of many traditional wedding customs. Despite the vintage early-1970s wedding photographs, the basic message of this book will never really go out of date—it's a classic. I especially recommend the chapter on pre-wedding planning. Look for it in libraries. Because it also deals with the socio-anthropological aspects and historical background of weddings, you may find it, as I did, in the library of your local university or community college.

Decision-making

Wedding planning often seems to consist of hundreds of small details that make up the whole. As you plan your wedding, you'll want to make decisions that reflect your values. When making a decision on something like guest list size or type of ceremony, it helps sometimes to step back and ask yourselves, what is the underlying decision we are making? For example, deciding whether or not to have a religious ceremony is usually more than a decision about whether to have your wedding in a house of worship. It may be a statement of the role religion will play in your marriage, or it may reflect the wishes of a parent or set of relatives you wish to please. A decision about wedding size can also be a decision about atmosphere—will it be an intimate family wedding, or a large affair?

Wedding planning can be a metaphor for decision-making in the future marriage. Making choices and compromises to please yourselves and others is part of the process. *How to Have the Wedding You Want,* by Danielle Claro (Berkley Books, 1995), helps couples pinpoint what is important to them in planning their wedding, and identifies signs of potential conflicts with relatives, so that couples can avoid or resolve problems.

Here is a list of things you might want to consider, in the approximate order in which you may need to do them. This is not a mold into which to fit your wedding. Depending on the nature of your situation, you may choose to omit some items altogether, or deal with them in a different sequence.

- Type of ceremony and size
- Ceremony and reception budget
- Time of day
- Reception
- Ceremony and reception date(s)
- Ceremony location—indoors or out
- Reception location and size, if different from ceremony
- Reserving ceremony and reception site(s)
- Guest list
- Invitations, response cards
- Attendants—number and type
- Ceremony—
    vows,
    readings,
    traditions and customs,
    guest/family participation,
    other elements

- Officiant
- Legal matters; marriage license, change of
  name, wills
- Planning for lifestyle changes—housing,
  finances, etc.
- Guest accommodations
- Honeymoon
- Food and beverages
- Music—ceremony and reception
- Photography/videography
- Wedding rings
- Wedding clothing
- Gifts
- Pre- or post-wedding parties
- Ceremony rehearsal/rehearsal dinner
- Transportation arrangements
- Decorations/decor
- Flowers
- Candles
- Guest book
- Favors/small gifts for guests
- Cleanup
    recycling
    nontoxic cleaning materials
    composting of fruit, vegetable and floral
        scraps

It is important to allow yourselves enough time
to plan and secure the services of various
professionals, or to delegate those tasks to friends
and relatives who are available and willing to
help you. Several months is not an unrealistic
amount of time to devote to wedding planning.
Some ceremony and reception sites are booked

months to a year or more in advance. Also, finding professionals willing to adapt to your green plans, or learning to do some things yourselves may take more research.

If you have lots of friends who are eager to help out, you can try having a work party eight to twelve weeks before the wedding. Cooks assemble and freeze the food that can be made ahead. Craft-minded people make paper for wedding favors, possibly invitations (see the appendix), and figure out how to arrange the flowers. Literary-minded folks write haiku for wedding favors. Organizationally talented people draft a plan for the ceremony rehearsal, if there will be one. Others can address invitations, make directional signs, design and draw a map to the site if necessary, etc.

In her book *I Do,* Sydney Barbara Metrick recommends that couples draw up a schedule for the ceremony, including preparations, and give a copy to everyone actively involved. We did this, and found it to be very helpful. Everyone knew exactly where we would be at a certain time, and what would happen in case of rain.

Wedding Timeline
This is a typical count-down schedule with some modifications, partially based on couples' experiences as compiled by the editors of Bride's magazine in their book,*Wedding Nightmares* (Plume, Penguin Books, 1993). (Read the book aloud for amusing entertainment at bridal showers—but not recommended for the faint of

heart.) Don't feel that this is the final word on wedding planning; make you own decisions based on the needs of your individual situation. Some people want a year and a half to plan; others prefer to marry in a month or two. I believe in doing things far ahead of time, in order to leave myself plenty of time to panic.

9 months before, or earlier:
• Determine wedding budget.
• Investigate and select wedding/reception site(s); reserve with deposit(s). Be sure to arrange to book the site for a rehearsal, if you will have one.
• Set date for ceremony/reception.
• Make general decisions about wedding size, type, number of guests, whether there will be attendants, whether you will have a theme or color scheme.
• Begin casually shopping in thrift shops, consignment stores, via newspaper ads, or at store sales for any wedding garb you need. Sales of end-of-season fashions can save you money. Look at patterns if you plan to make your own outfit, or engage a professional immediately if you want something handmade, but don't sew.

8 months before:
• Finalize guest list.
• Decide whether you will have a catered reception, fancy potluck reception, will do the food yourself with help from friends and family, or even have food at all. Depending on your decision, begin making arrangements with friends

and family, or choose a caterer, sign a contract, and leave a deposit.
• Begin researching material for your vows, if you are writing your own.

7 months before:
• Finalize reception menu.
• Choose beverage for toasting. Find distributors if you're doing your own food, and make arrangements to order enough.
• Begin shopping antique stores and pawn shops for wedding rings, or see jewelers about resetting existing jewelry, if you don't like it in its current form.

6 months before:
• Do research and make travel arrangements for honeymoon trip.
• Audition musicians and finalize your choices of music and musicians for ceremony and reception.
• Decide who your attendants will be, and what they will wear.

5 months before:
• Choose and make arrangements with your officiant.
• Select invitations, order, and have them printed or begin hand writing them.
• Hire a photographer, or ask a talented friend to take wedding photos of you as a wedding gift. You supply the film and pay for the developing.
• Finalize music selections with musicians.
• Purchase/make arrangements for attendants' attire.

4 months before:
• Purchase and wrap attendants' gifts in recycled paper, or see*The New Green Christmas* for some other ideas.
• Decide where to hold the rehearsal dinner, if you have one, and find out how far in advance arrangements must be made.

3 months before:
• Determine lodging arrangements for out-of-town guests.
• Have a wedding work party. Prepare and freeze make-ahead reception food.
• Make wedding favors. Make maps for wedding and reception location(s).
• Organize wedding day schedule, including ceremony and reception preparations.
• Delegate responsibility of various tasks to trustworthy individuals.

2 months before:
• Mail out invitations.
• Make sure you have all your wedding clothing and accessories in hand, including underwear, shoes and hosiery, and that everything fits. It will greatly help your peace of mind.
• If you like, have wedding rings engraved inside with your names and wedding date, or have one another's rings engraved inside with a special message that you won't see until your wedding day. Until then, keep the rings in a safe deposit box, or you'll be tempted to read your messages beforehand!

1 month before:
• Get the marriage license, or at least inquire about your state's requirements, so you don't discover the day before the wedding that your state has a mandatory 3-day waiting period.
• Get attendants' attire to them, unless it is being rented.

2 weeks before:
• Assemble nonperishable wedding cake ingredients and equipment.
• Get final version of your vows to officiant.
• As wedding gifts arrive, open them, write and address thank-you notes immediately, and set the notes aside to mail as soon as the wedding is over.

1 week before:
• Give a final head count to caterer.

3 days before:
• Take frozen reception food out of freezer and put into refrigerator to defrost.
• Buy perishable wedding cake ingredients.

2 days before:
• Bake cake, allow to cool.
• Visit with out-of-town guests.

1 day before:
• Frost cake or cover with marzipan and decorate with piped frosting or edible flowers (not Soy Kaas, though; you'll need to do that tomorrow).
• Pick up flowers from your supplier, or collect them from friends who are supplying them.

- Chill beverages.
- Prepare salads, fruit salads.
- Hold wedding rehearsal, if you have one.
- Have rehearsal dinner afterwards.

The Day:
- Arrange flowers. Includes bouquets, bouton-nieres, corsages, flower girl baskets, altar and table arrangements.
- Frost cake with Soy Kaas cream cheese frosting, if that is the type you chose.
- Depart for the wedding site with all your wedding clothing, wallet and checkbook, guest book and pen, flowers, food and cake. It helps if you've delegated some of these tasks.
- Get married.
- Have your photographs taken some time today.
- Thank everyone who helped.
- Pay musicians, caterer, site manager, officiant, lodgings manager.
- Drop those thank-you notes in the mail, and write others as soon as you get home.
- Relax.

Chapter Two: Invitations

One of the simplest green things you can do for your wedding is to choose recycled paper wedding invitations, response cards (if you use them), and thank-you notes that are recyclable. Professional wedding consultants usually know which companies manufacture invitations with recycled paper content. Most stationers carry lines of recycled paper—blank cards, note paper, etc., whether or not they are in a special section of the store. You may have to read the backs of cards and stationery boxes to determine which have recycled paper content. The higher the percentage of recycled paper fibers, either pre- or postconsumer, the better. Paper that is unbleached, or bleached without chlorine is good, also. Here are some suggestions:

Stamps
• Choose traditional moisten-and-stick postage stamps in sheets or cardstock booklets. The sheets don't have packaging (unless it's a glassine paper envelope—recyclable), and the booklets are recyclable. The self-adhesive stamps come with a nonrecyclable plastic sheet backing, which makes them less desireable.

Pens
Fountain pens
• Invest in a good quality fountain pen, and as you use up all your old throwaway ballpoint and cartridges, don't get any more disposables! Avoid nonrefillable fountain pen cartridges, also. You can use fountain pens to address (or even write— see below) wedding invitations, for the guest book, to write haiku wedding favors (see chapter 9), and as gifts for attendants. In a more gracious era, fountain pens were second only to the pocket watch as the preferred men's gift. Owner Pier Gustafson of **The Good Service Pen Company** collects and repairs fountain pens from the 1920s and 30s, when they were made to last. Pens often had a lifetime guarantee before the days of planned obsolescence. The green advantages to using a vintage pen are the good quality, and the fact that you are reusing an item. Prices begin at around $20; the median price for a modest pen is around $30. The Good Service Pen Company, 1 Fitchburg Street, Somerville, MA 02143; phone (617) 666-2975. Antique stores are also another source for vintage fountain pens.

If you opt for a modern fountain pen, purchase one with an ink converter, a reservoir with a tiny pump-action lever for drawing ink into the barrel. Check at art and office supply stores. For other fountain pens, check the Seventh Generation, Earth Care and The Natural Choice catalogs.

Glass pens
Another option is a dip-style glass pen. The ink is held in fluted edges of the tip. These pens can

use water-soluble ink, and have no throwaway parts; the glass bottles of ink can be recycled, and the metal caps be recycled as scrap metal. As an extra benefit, they are hand-formed of strong, borosilicate glass (Pyrex), and can be shipped back for repairs (I stupidly broke the tip off my pen, and they cheerfully repaired it for a very minimal fee). They are a lovely way to combine function with art; they come in various colors and grip sizes. Each glass pen comes with a clear glass pen rest and a bottle of ink. The price range when I purchased mine was $75 to $85—actually quite competitive with good-quality new fountain pens. Contact Michael and Sheila Ernst, 6237 Hwy. 38, Drain, OR 97435; (503) 836-7637.

Invitation options

• Check the most recent *National Green Pages* for recycled paper products. It is available through some newsstands and Co-op America. See the catalog list in the Resources section at the back of this book.

• **Found Stuff PaperWorks** is one of three companies I've located that have wonderfully creative, beautiful handmade recycled fiber papers from a variety of materials. Theirs include dried flowers, cotton, onion skins and linen. They print wedding invitations on their paper, using soy inks and letterpress printing. Found Stuff PaperWorks, 744 G Street, Studio 201, San Diego, CA 92101; (619) 338-9432.

• **Langdell Paperworks** also makes handmade paper, and does lots of wedding invitations. They specialize in handmade cotton fiber paper with flower petals. Other variants include a paper with banana leaf fiber and flowers, and another from locally-grown corn leaf fibers. They also make two types of journals suitable for wedding guest books, and will print custom invitations. Langdell Paperworks, R.R. #2 Box 1191, Plot Road, Johnson, VT 05656; (802) 644-6647.

• **Oblation Papers & Press** makes wedding invitations of handmade cotton paper with wild-flowers, and prints them on a letterpress. They also make acid-free photo albums with recycled pages, guest books, notecards, and a papermaking kit. Brochure available. Oblation Papers & Press, 6503 SW Luana Beach Road, Vashon Island, WA 98070; 1-800-99-0748 or (360) 463-1974.

• When you look at invitations in catalogs at stationers' and printers', check for a section devoted to recycled paper. Select invitations made of real paper; avoid stationery with foil envelope inserts, or with plasticized or overly shiny paper, as these will not recycle.

• If you're adventurous and enjoy being creative, you can make your own recycled paper as an art form for wedding invitations, response cards, even wedding favors (see chapter 9 for wedding favor ideas). The smallest size of postcard or envelope the post office will take is 3 1/2" x 5." See the appendix for instructions for making attractive recycled paper yourself.

• For a small wedding, consider a handwritten personal note (written with a fountain or glass pen, of course!) on beautiful recycled paper stationery. According to Emily Post, this is the most flattering sort of invitation to receive, and you'll probably get a better response rate.

• Many printers now use vegetable-based inks, which are more environmentally benign than conventional printing inks. Ask around.

• Be creative with available recycled paper stationery resources. For our invitations we chose blank cards with an illustration that looked like our outdoor wedding site. For response cards, we found solid color pastel note cards and envelopes that matched tones in the invitation. Maps to wedding and receptions sites printed on recycled 8" x 11" paper were also included. The weightier invitation "packet" cost us extra in postage, however.

• An alternative to paper invitations is to telephone guests. This works best with a smaller wedding. To put your long distance phoning dollars to work for the environment, use a long distance service such as Earth Tones or Working Assets. For further information on them, call or write:

Earth Tones—the Environmental Phone Company: Customer Service: 1-800-466-1550 P.O. Box 547, Noblesville, IN 46060-0547.

Working Assets Long Distance, Customer Service, P.O. Box 2024, Mechanicsburg, PA 17055-0764; 1-800-788-0898.

Both companies used recycled paper and send a newsletter about environmental legislative developments and other information with each bill.

Basic wedding invitation format

You can be as creative as you want, but an invitation should contain wording that clearly informs the guests that a wedding (to which they are invited) will take place.

• bride and groom's names
• parents' names (optional)
• wording that makes it clear that the guests are invited, and clearly states whether they are invited to the wedding, the reception, or both
• date, time, and place of wedding
• information about the time and location of the reception, possibly also the type, for example:

Brunch reception immediately following (or the exact time if not right away)
The Clearview Hall
2727 Recycle Lane
Anytown, Anystate

• optional—a map and/or written directions to the wedding and reception sites, particularly if they are hard to find. This is especially helpful to out-of-town guests.
• response card and envelope—optional, but very useful in getting a commitment from guests so that you can plan reception food, seating arrangements for the ceremony and reception, and possible lodging for out-of-town guests. It is helpful if you stamp the envelope. Unbelievably, many people today seem to have trouble interpreting this standard response card:

M_____   will____   attend.

Number in party_____.

Some couples have received response cards back with no name, or no number in party, or both. For our wedding invitation, we devised the following response card:

_____   will____
(name)

will not_____ attend. Number in party _____.

For those guests who sent their response cards back, everyone completed them correctly.
• optional—sentiment appropriate to the occasion (short line of poetry, or a quote about love, commitment, marriage)—when present, usually on the cover of the invitation.

Chapter 3: Choosing a wedding or reception site

There are advantages to having your ceremony and reception at the same place. You save transportation fuel and reduce pollution.

The time of day is something else to consider. Traditionally, the later in the day the ceremony took place, the more formal the wedding was considered to be. Regardless of traditional notions of formality and informality dictating the time the ceremony is held, if you have your ceremony during daylight hours, you will save on electricity to light the location—unless you've chosen a windowless building. If you've selected an outdoor location, chances are that you will want your guests to see it in daylight. For evening ceremonies, candlelight as a light source is very romantic (have fire extinguishers handy), and saves on electricity as well. See Chapter 9 for types of environmentally friendly candles and alternatives.

If you are looking for wedding sites and don't know quite how or where to begin, one way is to check wedding announcements in the local newspaper for ideas. You'll find out what locations are conventional and available for weddings, and you may find out about a few unique places that might not have otherwise occurred to you. This perusal of the paper can be ongoing as you use other methods.

Other resources are: the classified pages of the phone book under Churches or Synagogues; Chambers of Commerce for information on facilities for use; regional guides, including historical landmark registries and even bed and breakfast guides (some of the more luxurious bed and breakfasts have great facilities for a small, family wedding); parks directories.

If you're in that area, the Saunders Hotel Group (see Accommodations in Chapter 10) has three hotels in Boston that are green hotels and offer wedding reception facilities and catering. They range in size from modest to large.

On the opposite coast is the Four Seasons Olympic in Seattle. They recycle extensively enough to merit an article in the May 1995 *Enviro* ("Record Recycling Rate," Kirk Gormley, pp. 16-17). See Accommodations in Chapter 10 for more details.

Check local or regional business publications to see which businesses are winning awards or being mentioned for their environmentally sound business practices. You may find the wedding location of your dreams among them.

Holding a wedding and/or reception in an ecologically sensitive area

What if you want to hold a wedding for 50 guests in a pristine wilderness area? Sometimes the best answer to this question is—just don't do it. One of the most intrusive outdoor wedding stories I have heard involves a couple who were married on a mountaintop. It was a roadless area with no trails. A helicopter flew the couple and guests there—how noisy and disturbing to wildlife!

Fortunately, your wedding won't be like that one, but there are some things to keep in mind. Many beautiful wild areas seem to beg for you to share them with others. The problem with bringing even a small group of people to completely isolated, untouched wilderness areas is that many of these areas are very fragile and susceptible to human footprints. For example, the heather in lovely alpine meadows takes a long time to grow; heather plants in Parks Service greenhouses grow just one inch every two years, and botanists believe it grows even more slowly in harsher climates. A plant just one foot tall may be many, many years old—and it doesn't take kindly to being trampled. Some native dune grasses can endure all kinds of surf and wind action, only to die if they are stepped upon. Wetlands also are very fragile. And wildlife shouldn't be fed by humans, either directly or indirectly through food accidentally dropped or left behind.

If you've both always wanted to be married in a pristine wilderness area with delicate vegetation and wildlife, the two of you can arrange to be married there at the toughest area of the site (a rock outcropping, for example) with an officiant and the minimum number of witnesses legally required (two in most states). Then you can have a reception later for a large crowd of guests in a location that can accommodate them.

An alternative is to use wilderness as a backdrop to your wedding, in national and state parks or national forests. A one-page article by Chris Theimer in *Sunset* magazine (August 1995, Northern California edition) has some good, solid tips to get you started.

A third option is to have your wedding in town, and decorate your reception site with enlarged photos of your chosen wilderness area. Use flowers and greenery similar to what grows there—ferns for an old-growth forest, heather for alpine meadows. This will get guests involved who, for whatever reason, might otherwise not be able to come to an outdoor wilderness wedding.

Reception Format

Some of the decisions about the location of your reception will be determined by the type of reception you wish to have. One way to cut down on waste and cost is to keep the size of your ceremony and reception small. Less is more. At an intimate gathering you have more opportunity to enjoy one another's company, and that of your guests. Consider a modest-sized guest list and a relaxed reception without a booming master of ceremonies or band music. The focus can be the two of you and your wedding. Guests can eat, talk with one another, listen to quality music by a few good musicians, and visit with you. If there is not a rigid agenda, you can cut and serve the cake, toss the bouquet and garter (if you have one), and leave when it seems best.

On the other hand, if you want a large guest list, then the simpler the reception is, the more people you can accommodate. If you're having a standup buffet reception with finger food, cake and punch, you'll have less preparation—and less cost per guest—than if you decide to have a formal sit-down dinner and dance afterwards (especially if you're doing most of it yourselves).

One couple I know wanted an intimate wedding without a lot of fuss. The night before their wedding, they had a rehearsal and a rehearsal dinner afterward for all the guests, and served wedding cake. This rehearsal dinner was a substitute for a reception. After their wedding on the following day, they greeted family and friends in the church foyer. They then changed clothes, waved goodbye, hopped in their car, and let the relatives continue visiting in the church. This was a perfect solution for them.

If you love to dance, you might consider contradancing at your reception, especially if your guests are in widely varying age groups. I attended a school dedication celebration where the talented dance band consisted of a guitarist, fiddle player, and singer/caller who instructed everyone, children and adults alike. Tired, bored adults soon were smiling and enjoying themselves thoroughly. The circle dances were simple enough for everyone there, including young children. It's a great way to get guests to mingle and participate. For instrumental groups and callers, check with folk music stores; often they have a bulletin board of musicians for hire.

Chapter   4: Ceremony

For creating your own ceremony, see the list of books mentioned under Planning in Chapter 1, especially *The Wedding Book* by Kirschenbaum and Stensrud; *I Do—A Guide to Creating Your Own Unique Wedding Ceremony,* by Metrick; Leviton's *Weddings By Design;* and Diamant's *The New Jewish Wedding.*

Most people enjoy searching for meaningful readings that will make their wedding unique. Religious writings, nature essays, poetry are all potential sources of special words for your wedding. You may want to begin by searching for topics in sources such as *Bartlett's Quotations,* and from there find the complete essay or poem of the writer whose quote pleases you.

Those who wish to incorporate a nature theme in their readings for a church—or outdoor— wedding may find the following Bible passages appropriate (the King James version is so poetic !):

- Song of Solomon 2:11-13
- Psalm 16: 1-6.
- Psalm 104, especially 1-13.
- For a mention of the ocean, see Psalm 107: 21, 23-25, 29, 30.
- Psalm 147: 1, 4, 5, 7-9, 15-18.
- Psalm 148: 1, 3-10, 13.

Here are some possible benedictions or ceremony closings:

• Isaiah 55: 12 For ye shall go out with joy, and be led forth with peace: the mountains and the hills shall break forth before you into singing, and all the trees of the field shall clap their hands.

• Revelation 7: 2, 3 And I saw another angel ascending from the east, having the seal of the living God: and he cried with a loud voice... saying, Hurt not the earth, neither the sea, nor the trees...

Two good anthologies of nature readings and poetry are *The Earth Speaks,* edited by Steve Van Matre and Bill Weiler, and *Earth Prayers,* edited by Elizabeth Roberts and Elias Amidon. See the bibliography at the back of this book for more information.

Chapter 5: Clothes

The choices you make in clothes for this day may not seem to have much of an impact on the environment. Actually, they do. The manufacture of clothing is a many-level process. You can choose beautiful clothes in a way that will not contribute to air pollution, water pollution or soil degradation, or will reduce those effects significantly.

Bride's
The traditional big, full-length, wedding gown is expensive, uses a lot of fabric, is often worn only once by one wearer, and requires dry cleaning on a grand scale. Dry cleaning releases Volatile Organic Compounds (VOC) into the air, creating air pollution. The VOC in the air leads eventually to lower ozone atmospheric levels (the "ozone hole" problem). Dry cleaning also puts hazardous chemicals into the water system. Despite the fact that solvent can be reprocessed or reclaimed, it seems best to use dry cleaning sparingly, if at all. Use cleaners' services for spot cleaning or to professionally press launderable clothes.

If the traditional, full-length wedding gown is something you cannot do without, there are some greener alternatives.

The traditional gown—green options

1) Borrow or rent a gown. This reuses resources, but still involves dry cleaning. If a borrowed gown is not dusty or dirty, but only has light staining or soiling around the sleeve cuffs, for example, it can be spot cleaned, which uses less solvent. *Choose to Reuse* (by Nikki and David Goldbeck, Woodstock, New York: Ceres Press, 1995) lists two businesses that specifically rent bridal and attendants' gowns.

2) The heirloom wedding gown. This also involves reuse of existing product, but will probably require dry cleaning. If it is a delicate vintage cotton fabric, see if the cleaners can simply launder and press it gently.

3) Purchase a secondhand gown from a consignment shop, antique shop, or thrift shop. This also eliminates the manufacturing cycle by reuse of existing products, but will probably involve dry cleaning. You may find charming vintage wedding clothes in good condition that a friend or family member can borrow in the future.

4) Have a gown made with washable fabric, or make it yourself, if you or a family member are accomplished at sewing. That way, if the garment becomes stained and needs to be borrowed or bequeathed, it can be washed at home with bio-degradable soap or detergent (see the Seventh Generation catalog if you can't find any locally),

and professionally pressed at a cleaner's. Be sure to check the laundering/cleaning instructions at the end of the fabric bolt before you buy. Rayon is usually labeled for dry cleaning because it wrinkles so much during washing, but if it is carefully hand washed in cold water, it can be pressed at home, or professionally pressed; experiment with a small swatch first. Even "dry clean only" silk can be hand washed in many cases—if it has been washed and preshrunk before being made into a garment. *Sensational Silk* by Gail Brown has directions for this, and sewing instructions. See the Resources section at the end of this chapter. If in doubt about a fabric, purchase a quarter of a yard of it, cut it in half, and try machine washing/drying and hand laundering/air drying the two pieces before you make the final purchase. Reuse the sample fabric to make a ring pillow, sachets, gift items, etc.

To take this option one step further, use a secondhand dress pattern. The good ones are distinctive, and you'll have a unique gown. Thrift shops sometimes have wonderful finds this way.

5) Instead of a wear-it-only-once veil, consider wearing your hair "up", or with flowers or a hat you will wear again. Back Porch Ivy is a source of custom-made hats and clothing made of natural and recycled fibers that are earth-friendly, including some beautiful gauzes. Back Porch Ivy, 28B Parker Way, Santa Barbara, CA 93101; phone (805) 963-8080.

Alternatives to the traditional gown

6) Purchase a dress that can be worn again, made of fabric that can be laundered at home.

7) Purchase a secondhand outfit that you can wear again that might not otherwise be considered for a wedding. This includes launderable matching silk blouse and skirt ensembles, and attractive dressy suits.

8) Make (or have made) a wear-again dress. Use the same guidelines as per Option 4 for traditional gowns.

Groom's

The dry cleaning problem exists for men's dress clothing also. Except for the protagonist of Anne Tyler's The *Accidental Tourist,* who began laundering his suits at home by treading them underfoot while in the shower, the concept of a launderable men's suit is as yet a thing of the future. Here are options for grooms and attendants:

1) Rent a tuxedo or suit. This is the usual approach to menswear in weddings. It involves dry cleaning.

2) Wear clothing you will wear again (or have worn before), of a color that does not show soil easily. Small staining on nonlaunderable clothes can be spot cleaned. Most men own a dark suit. The groom and male attendants can be given matching ties and pocket handkerchiefs to wear and keep; these can match the colors of the women attendants' dresses.

3) If you're the careful, considerate type not likely to spill food or drink on it, borrow a tuxedo

from a relative or friend. Professional musicians often own at least one, but they use them for work, so you need to be sure you can return a tuxedo or tails in perfect condition.

4) Purchase a secondhand suit, tuxedo, or tails from a consignment store, antique shop, or thrift shop. A jeweler we spoke with told us that he found the tuxedo for his wedding in a secondhand store. It looked remarkably like the one worn by his grandfather in a turn-of-the-century wedding photo. Again, this will involve dry cleaning, but someone may borrow that suit in the future, or it can be resold.

5) Have a suit or outfit made with washable fabric (or make it yourself, if you or a family member are accomplished at sewing). See Option 4 under the bride's section for suggestions. Two companies that make and sell vintage and ethnic patterns for men and women are Harper House and FOLKWEAR. See the Resources section at the end of this chapter.

Attendants'

Attendants' outfits should definitely be something washable that they can wear again, especially if they are paying for them. Renting attendants' formal wear is also a good option. Jandi Classics specializes in formal gown rental. Their gowns are made of machine-washable taffeta, so renters can feel good about both the reuse of the gown, and about avoiding drycleaning. See the Bridal Gowns and Formal Wear articles in *Choose to Reuse* for information on their local dealers.

If you have a flower girl or ring bearer, ask their parents if the children already have clothes that are appropriate for a wedding. Children who regularly attend church or other dressy functions often have suitable clothes already in the closet. The flower girl may have a dress in colors that will match the bridal attendants' dresses. The ring bearer may already have a suit and tie.

Natural/organically-grown   fibers
To take the concept a little further, consider making wedding clothes out of natural fiber fabric. Natural fibers such as cotton, linen, wool, silk, and even hemp linen are washable, biodegradable, renewable resources, unlike synthetic fibers made from petroleum-based chemicals. When they are organically grown and processed without harmful chemicals such as formaldehyde or chlorine, these textiles are the best of both worlds. See *The Green Consumer* and *Nontoxic, Natural, & Earthwise* for further discussion of the procedures, pesticides and chemicals commonly used to grow and process various natural fibers.

For the bride and groom who want dressy wedding clothing of organically grown, natural fibers, there are two routes to go: purchase the fabric and have it made or make it yourself; or find a designer who uses organic or recycled fiber fabrics.

Fabric sources
These are a few of the sources available. Check the National Green Pages for others.

• Ocarina Textiles makes fabrics with FoxFibre™ organically grown, colored cotton. This type of cotton actually grows in a range of colors, from medium brown to white to a light medium green. Each order is custom woven. Textile patterns are two-toned in white and colored cotton, and range from plain to herringbone, chevron, and several diamond-shapes. This type of fabric could work well with a man's summer suit, or made into ethnic or folkwear-based clothing for men and women. See Harper House and FOLKWEAR in the Resources section for suitable patterns. They also sell a variety of natural material buttons, including tagua nut. See the Resources section at the back of this chapter for their address.

• The Ohio Hempery, Inc., sells hemp linen and hemp linen/cotton or silk blends. I was very impressed with the fabric samples I received. The hemp is grown without chemical pesticides or herbicides, and the non-fiber parts of the plant are plowed back into the soil to recycle nutrients (the term is "field retted"). See the Resources section at the back of this chapter for their address.

It might seem that cotton or linen isn't a suitable fabric for wedding clothes. On the contrary! For the individual who wants to sew his or her own wedding clothes, there are vintage patterns and sewing techniques that work well with cotton and other natural fibers, and make fine natural fiber fabric look dressy. The Ohio Hempery notes that hemp fabric is authentic for period costumes, which leads us to a further discussion of vintage patterns. If you've seen old photographs of turn-of-the-century tea gowns made of cotton batiste, or antique dresses made of delicate cotton lace, you're probably aware that cotton can be used to make exquisitely delicate and lovely dresses and even lingerie (camisoles, nightgowns, etc.). This type of sewing, that uses tiny pin tucks and lace and embroidery insets, is called French Heirloom sewing. French Heirloom sewing is used for natural fibers only, such as fine cotton lawn or batiste, linen, or silk broadcloth. There are books and magazines available that teach the techniques, and sewing books often include sections on French Heirloom. See the Resources section at the end of this chapter.

Basically, any pattern can be sewn in the French Heirloom style simply by using the techniques to insert lace and other trim and make pintucks. In the Special Occasions 1993 edition of *Sew Beautiful* magazine, there is an article, entitled "An Old-Fashioned Gown," by a reader-contributor who made her own gown with cotton batiste and these techniques. It's a gorgeous Civil War-era gown, formal enough for almost any type of wedding, yet refreshingly new. Because she made it to be an heirloom, wearable by others, it has a loose-fitting blouson type bodice and gathered skirt with an inner cotton drawstring (because the rubber in elastic eventually disintegrates with time). The detail is exquisite. If you aren't proficient at sewing, this would be the type of project to give to a professional dressmaker.

Both FOLKWEAR and Harper House have vintage patterns, including patterns for vintage wedding clothes or clothes suitable for adaptation, and FOLKWEAR has ethnic patterns as well. FOLKWEAR has an Edwardian bridal gown pattern with full instructions for heirloom-type sewing and three versions of the dress. Harper House has wedding gown patterns from garments dating from 1885, 1907, 1930 and 1939. See the Resources section at the end of this chapter.

Even if vintage patterns aren't for you, beautiful wedding clothes can still be made of natural fiber fabrics. Consider how lovely fine cotton Venetian lace is—or good quality, real 100 percent cotton eyelet.

Clothing sources

• Cannabis Clothes sells the components of a man's suit—sport coat, "baggy pants" (trousers) and vest—in a natural, monochromatic herringbone hemp linen. Their brochure states that colors are extra, so that is an option, too. They do custom orders, also. Cannabis Clothes, P. O. Box 1167, Occidental, CA 95465; phone (707) 874-1104.

• Crucial Creations also sells trousers, vests and sport jackets in hemp fabric. See the 1996 *National Green Pages* for a picture. Crucial Creations, 4550 South 12th Avenue, #111, Tuscon, AZ 85714; phone (520) 682-0725 or 1-800-HEMP-4-US (that's 1-800-436-7487).

• Another source is Worldware in San Francisco. Owner and president Shari Sant designs wedding clothes and bridesmaids' dresses in sophisticated styles with organic or recycled fibers. Sant, who was Design Director with Ralph Lauren for 9 years, chooses organic and recycled fibers for their lesser impact on the earth, and uses a local seamstress rather than overseas labor— less fossil fuel used in shipping, no exploitation of overseas workers. For more information, call (415) 487-9030.

• Back Porch Ivy has natural and recycled fiber clothing and hats. See Option 5 under Bride's clothes at the beginning of this chapter for the address and phone number.

• Also, from time to time, check various catalogs that have clothing. Some issues have more garment items to choose from than others, but you may find what you're looking for in an unexpected source.

As with other organically-grown and recycled content products, when the demand increases, more products will become available.

Shoes—Men and Women

Before you buy any additional shoes, look in your closet. There may be a pair that would be suitable for your wedding. If not, and you decide to buy new shoes, make sure that they are something you can wear again, are in a style that will not become dated soon, and are of sufficient quality so that they will last awhile.

If you are a dancer, consider wearing dance shoes with your wedding ensemble. After the wedding, these can get lots of mileage. Brides with an ankle, floor, or ballet-length dress might wear white ballet slippers. Men could wear jazz oxfords if the floor surface is not damaging to the shoe soles. The Garnet Hill Spring 1995 catalog had elegant-looking white kid ballet slippers with Venetian lace appliqués, which were intended as bedroom slippers. For a similar effect, use white ballet shoes, remove the elastic instep strap and attach a lace appliqué over each shoe toe with rubber cement. That way, the appliqués can be easily removed after the wedding.

If you decide to buy second hand shoes, inspect them for wear and odor. Try them on with socks or stockings, and if you purchase them, wipe the insides with a clean rag moistened in hydrogen peroxide and let them dry out before wearing them.

Rings

Mining generates toxic waste that needs to be disposed of somewhere. Use existing already-mined precious metals and/or gemstones for your wedding rings (and engagement ring, too, if you decide to have one) in one or a combination of these ways:

• heirloom jewelry: these pieces can be simple, beautiful, unusual.

• estate jewelry, often sold by auctioneers or the jewelry departments of upscale department stores by special sale. Sometimes advertised in the newspaper, or you can phone to ask when the next sale will be.

• used jewelry from pawn shops or antique shops. Newspaper classifieds sometimes advertise used wedding rings, but be careful—get an appraisal from a certified jeweler.

• existing jewelry from any those sources, recast by a jeweler/designer into new items.

Obviously, jewelry recast uses more energy to produce it than simply using the rings as they are, but you're still avoiding the mining cycle.

Scratched used jewelry can be polished by a jeweler to restore its shininess, if it does not have an engraved pattern that might be worn off.

Avoid jewelry cleaner in little plastic jars, each with its own tiny brush. Instead, soak rings with gemstones (not pearls) in vinegar for about five minutes, scrub gently with an old discarded toothbrush, and rinse with warm water. This will remove soap deposits and skin oils from the undersides of gemstones. For more stubborn dirt, use biodegradable liquid dish detergent (the stuff for handwashing dishes), scrub gently with the toothbrush, and rinse with warm water. In *Clean & Green* , Annie Berthold-Bond has three recipes for gold cleaners, including one for gold jewelry.

Accessories

Use jewelry or accessories you already own, or can borrow. Or purchase them at an antique or second hand shop. If you buy something new, invest some thought beforehand and make sure your purchase will have a more positive impact. For example, tagua nuts are now being used as sustainable rainforest products. They look like ivory, and are made into jewelry, buttons, and other items by native forest peoples, who profit by our purchases. If you were to purchase a tagua nut necklace instead of one made of real or faux pearls, you'd be doing the rainforest and its inhabitants a better turn (a portion of all earnings goes to rainforest preservation). For tagua nut necklaces, check The Natural Choice, Earth Care and Seventh Generation catalogs. For tagua nut buttons, see the entry for Ocarina Textiles in the Fabric Sources section.

Instead of disposable paper tissues, use cotton handkerchiefs. They're reusable and cut down on landfill trash. You can find fine handkerchiefs in gift shops (usually more expensive), or in the hosiery departments (men's and women's) of better department stores. For vintage antique lace hankies, check in antique shops and vintage clothing stores.

For men, dress socks can be made of natural fibers such as silk, or wool or cotton. When most of us think of women's dress hosiery, we usually think of nylon stockings—make of petroleum-based nylon, a nonrenewable resource. The more environmentally friendly alternatives are wool tights, which are fine for winter and floor length dresses, or cotton blend tights. Cotton and wool blend tights come in neutral colors like off white, taupe, brown and black. Check department stores, or see the Garnet Hill catalog for tights and stockings that are cotton or wool blends. When your old nylon stockings wear out (or your cotton or wool ones), use them as stuffing for children's toys.

Personal care
Products for personal care can be among the most overpackaged items we consume. There is a multitude of cosmetics, soaps, shampoos, hair

conditioners, toothpastes, deodorants, disposable razors, each with its own (for now) nonrecyclable container. Many companies now make an effort to reduce packaging, or to package products in recycled materials, or to make them available in bulk. It is up to all of us to support this trend by purchasing products from these progressive manufacturers. However, the point is to try to consume fewer products and less packaging, not more, so use up the old products completely first, so that you create less waste of materials.

Other things to look for in good products is whether they contain nontoxic ingredients, use processing methods that are earth-friendly, and avoid animal testing.

To locate products and retailers that are earth-friendly and have made a commitment to the environment, see the *National Green Pages* .

A good consumer's guide for virtually any kind of purchasing you do is *Shopping for a Better World*. There are ratings for small and large companies, including gas and oil companies. The ratings include information on companies' performances in the areas of charitable giving, environmentally sound practices, family benefits, equal opportunity, investment in local communities, and other categories. *The Green Supermarket Shopping Guide* by John F. Wasik is another valuable resource that looks at the environmental claims of more than 200 companies, and rates products individually.

For an excellent book that describes and lists chemicals to avoid, and environmentally-benign products and where to find them, see Debra Lynn

Dadd's *Nontoxic, Natural & Earthwise*. This book is a vital resource.

Water conservation is important. If you don't have water conservation devices such as low-flow shower heads and faucet aerators installed already, do so now. Check the Seventh Generation and Real Goods catalogs.

If you have dry skin and hair and your area's water system is purified with chlorine, try a chlorine filter for your shower. These filters generally work with a low-flow shower head. Chlorine is very drying to the skin and hair, and is also absorbed through the skin during hot showers—not beneficial. I've been using a chlorine shower filter for over a year, and although no one has asked me if I've had a facelift or hair transplant, I notice that my skin is no longer as dry and itchy, and I've stopped needing my leave-in hair conditioner. Available through the Real Goods catalog and Global Environmental Technologies, 1-800-800-8377. G. E. T. will give you a 10% discount on a new filter when you return the used one to them for recycling.

Use biodegradable shampoos available in bulk (bring your own container) at food co-ops, or buy a huge bottle (hairdresser size, usually available at salons, beauty supply shops, or discount warehouses) and pour some into your old smaller bottle. This avoids excess packaging. Nature's Gate is a longstanding brand of shampoo that is both organic and biodegradable. It is usually sold in co-ops and health food stores. For soap, choose those that are biodegradable, such as castile. Many food co-ops and health food stores carry liquid soaps in bulk, or unwrapped soaps; these save on packaging.

Many fine calcium-based or baking soda-based toothpastes are sold in health food stores and even regular grocery stores (Tom's of Maine seems to be sold about everywhere). My personal choice of tooth care product is plain old Arm & Hammer baking soda, because it comes in a recyclable cardboard box made of recycled cardboard. Sometimes to jazz up the taste, I mix 1 teaspoon ground cloves with 3 tablespoons baking soda, which is a 10% mixture of cloves. The disadvantage to this is that it turns my toothbrush bristles brown, and sometimes bits of cloves remain in my teeth. Also, baking soda is too abrasive for some people, and individuals on a low sodium diet should probably avoid it.

Toothbrushes with replaceable bristles (so that you save the handle for reuse) are a great invention. Try your local co-op or health food store; also see the Seventh Generation and Natural Choice catalogs.

For any personal care products, avoid aerosol cans like the plague that they are. If you feel that you must use hairspray (and think of this: the majority of people in the world don't), use one with a pump action and a refillable bottle made of recyclable plastic. Instead of aerosol shaving cream, use a mug, shaving brush and bio-degradable soap. Avoid disposable razors; buy a razor with replaceable blades instead. The metal blades could be recyclable as scrap metal; check with local recyclers. Check The Natural Choice, Earth Care and Seventh Generation catalogs, and the November and December issues of *E, The Environmental Magazine* for razors with replaceable blades. Even better, if you can find one, is a wind-up clockwork shaver. You save water, batteries, electricity, and avoid the aerosol question altogether.

Instead of lip salve or moisturizer in tiny throwaway dispensers, try making your own with coconut oil and beeswax purchased in bulk from a natural foods store. I can purchase beeswax very inexpensively in unwrapped muffin-like shapes at my local food co-op. If you can't find a source, try a beekeeper. The coconut oil should also be available from natural food stores. In a heavy saucepan over medium-low heat, melt one part beeswax and two to three parts coconut oil; use the greater concentration of beeswax for winter conditions, skiing, etc. Pour into small screwtop containers; these can be clean, empty containers of lip salve, or newly purchased from a pharmacy—you'll simply save them to reuse for the next batch. I also have saved old roll-up lip moisturizer tubes and washed them with hot water and dish detergent, and filled them with my homemade lip moisturizer. This moisturizer has only two ingredients, very minimal packaging, works well, is colorless, and smells faintly of honey.

Most health food stores carry natural-ingredient stick or roll-on deodorants instead of aerosols. For its minimal packaging and refills available in recyclable glass bottles, Tom's of Maine roll-on deodorant is the most environmentally sound of any deodorant I've found. Check health food stores and co-ops first. Tom's of Maine, P.O. Box 710 Kennebunk, Maine 04043. They are a green company. Also see the list of deodorants in *Nontoxic, Natural, & Earthwise.*

Avoid the use of perfumes with animal musk. Instead, choose herbal or floral essential oils with no animal ingredients or testing.

Garden Botanika has natural cosmetics and body care products with moderate prices and botanical ingredients. Another feature is minimal packaging. The company has stores in malls in Portland, Oregon, and the greater Seattle area. See the catalog listings in the Resources section at the back of this book.

The Body Shop has natural body care products packaged in plastic bottles that are refillable in the store. They have over 80 stores in the United States. See the catalog listings in the Resources section at the back of this book.

Again, health food stores and natural food co-ops often have a variety of natural cosmetics, bulk lotions and shampoos. See the *National Green Pages* and *Nontoxic, Natural, & Earthwise* for information on products and how to order them if they are unavailable locally.

Hair Care

Hair dye

Avoid conventional dyes, which have been found to be carcinogenic. Use henna products instead, available at health food stores and co-ops. These are available in a wide range of colors, from pale blonde to red to dark brown and black.

Another alternative is to make some of the natural, nontoxic hair dyes in *Nontoxic, Natural & Earthwise.*

Curling your hair

Permanent waves contain ammonia, which is naturally-occurring, but takes a lot of energy to produce in the form in which we use it. Ammonia is not benign; try breathing the fumes from a typical beauty salon. In addition to fumes, the ammonia solution is rinsed down the drain into the water supply during the perming process. I find it significant that the first "green hair salon" does not do perms (Elemental in Albany, California; mentioned in the July-Aug. 1993 issue of *E Magazine*). Alternatives are electric rollers and curling irons, and old-fashioned hair curling methods such as pin curls, rollers and rag curls. Electric methods are fine for a rush job, but they require electricity, may damage permed, dry or very fine hair, and don't always give quite the curl you expected. They also almost always require hairspray to retain the curl. Rollers of any kind tend to leave a line where the curl starts. For my money, the best two methods of hair curling are good, old-fashioned pin curls and rag curls, and the one I favor is rag curls. Why? Because rag curls:

1) involve the reuse of a resource (clean rags or sewing scraps);
2) are reusable (as curlers again or as stuffing for a child's toy);
3) do not damage hair

4) are absolutely safe—no negative effects on
    health or environment
5) require no electricity—no accidental facial
    burns, either
6) hold until you wash your hair
7) cost absolutely nothing
8) are painless.

To set hair with rag curls, assemble lots of clean
rag scraps, usually laundered sewing scraps. The
rags work best if they are at least six inches long
and a half an inch to an inch wide. (They get
scrunched up, but if they're too thin, they fray and
wear out with repeated use and washings.) Take
a combed swatch of hair about an inch wide and
an eighth of an inch thick or less. Cheat by
putting the rag an inch from the end of your hair
and rolling hair ends around the rag. Continue
twisting the rag to roll your hair up to the desired
distance from your scalp. If you want curl that
starts from the top of your head, roll nearly to the
scalp (this is too lumpy for me to sleep on; I prefer
leaving the top four inches straight). If your hair
will be pulled back for your wedding hairstyle,
roll hair only to your ears. Roll the rest of your
hair. Now sleep on it. For an idea of how it
should look, see the 1994 movie remake of *Little
Women.* Amy has her hair in rag curls in one
scene. Try this a few times before your wedding
day so that you have practice doing it; you don't
want a "surprise" hairstyle.

Other alternatives to perms and electric curlers
include leaving the hair as it is (what a concept!);

pinning it into a bun with a few fresh flowers; wrapping or tying a scarf around it; or tucking it up under a hat. *Nontoxic, Natural, & Earthwise* lists one company that makes "natural" perms for home use; even those contain natural spirits of ammonia.

Nail care

The lowly nail clipper is really quite wonderful. Made of high quality stainless steel with an attached combination steel nail file and cuticle tool, it is inexpensive, durable, and lasts virtually forever. There are no empty bottles of fume-generating, toxic nail polish or polish remover to throw away, no disposable emery boards to toss. You don't need to schedule expensive and time-consuming nail appointments and touch-ups, coordinate nail polish colors with attendants' outfits and lipstick colors, or glue on disposable artificial nails. It is the ultimate green grooming accessory for men and women—and you can use it to cut loose threads off of clothes when you don't have scissors.

Natural, healthy nails are attractive, especially if not excessively long. If you have nail or hand problems due to extremely rough work, you may want to select wedding clothes that will be complemented by gloves. Men can wear tails, top hat and gloves, and women can choose from a variety of short and long gloves styles in lace or plain cotton—the vintage clothing sections of some antique shops are good sources for quality, recycled gloves.

Feminine hygiene

Feminine menstrual products are, like disposable diapers, thrown away with the naive hope that, if they're out of sight, they don't exist anymore. Most women and custodians have discovered that tampons often clog plumbing, and need to be thrown in the trash, not down the toilet. Paper pads have a plastic liner that will not biodegrade, and most things in landfills are not breaking down as quickly as we'd like, if at all. Plastic tampon applicators are flushed down the toilet, only to reappear on beaches (according to *The Green Consumer*, they're known as "New Jersey seashells" in some areas of the country). These problems don't even touch upon the harmful effects of paper processing to the environment, or the use of bleaches on the products to make them white. It has been suggested that the chlorine used to whiten tampons may be responsible for uterine and cervical cancer, not to mention the hazards it presents to the external environment.

The solution to this seems to be a return to the way things were before the advent of disposable pads. Several companies now make rewashable, reusable cotton menstrual pads in a wide range of sizes, styles and thicknesses. Since we're already returning to cloth diapers for babies, this seems like the next logical step. Like cloth diapers, they require an initial investment, but the money is recouped over time as you no longer spend it each month on disposables. Here is a list of a few of the products available. A bidet is very useful in conjunction with pads, and when used every other day in place of a daily shower, can be a nice water conservation item at other times.

Pads
• **Glad Rags** uses an oval-shaped envelope in bright abstract flannel print that encloses up to two flannel pads inside, and snaps around underwear crotch. Keepers!, P.O. Box 12751, Portland, OR 97212; (503) 282-0436.
• **Many Moons** has cotton flannel pads in florals or wild prints, and organic unbleached cotton pads. Many Moons, #14-130 Dallas Road (1), Victoria, B.C. V8V 1A3; (604) 382-1588.
• **Natural Concepts** makes a full line of pads, liners and accessories. Their system uses Velcro strips on pad bottoms and sewn into cotton underwear to secure the pads. The pads are unbleached cotton fleece (a luxurious flannel), and the Velcro is optional but necessary. Keema & Company, 2429 23rd St. SW, Brier, WA 98036. (206) 483-7186.
• **New Cycle** makes three styles of pads in two types of fabric: floral flannel pads (ordinary cotton); and organic cotton knit fabric, grown and produced without pesticides, bleaches or dyes. New Cycle, Inc. P.O. Box 1775, Sebastopol, CA 95473.
• *How to Live Green, Cheap and Happy* has directions for making homemade pads. The concept is good; just omit the cotton fiber, which gets thrown away after one use. See the bibliography at the back of this book for author and publisher information.

For travel and times when you lack laundry facilities, disposables may be the best solution.

• **Seventh Generation** makes disposable paper pads and liners that are free of both chlorine and fragrance. See the Catalogs section of the bibliography at the back of this book.

For those who prefer conventional brands of disposable pads and tampons, see *Nontoxic, Natural, and Earthwise,* or *Shopping for a Better World.* Just keep in mind that disposables don't simply go away.

Finally, avoid disposable douches. Most women's health care specialists agree that douching is not necessary.

Contraception

Probably the most environmentally friendly method of birth control, when used properly, is the ovulation method. There are no devices, nothing to throw away, no chemicals or containers, no packaging. It requires abstinence during the fertile days of a woman's cycle. It is not the same as the rhythm method, which is based on the calendar, not physiology. The ovulation method is best taught by a teacher who is experienced in the method herself. Denise Guren and Nealy Gillete have written an informative, reasonably-priced book, *The Ovulation Method: Cycles of Fertility,* which is a good adjunct to a course in the method. The book can be ordered through Denise Guren, 2908 Cottonwood, Bellingham, WA 98225. (206) 733-2044. The price is $3.95; Washington state residents add sales tax.

Your local Planned Parenthood office should be able to tell you if there is a teacher of the ovulation method in your area.

Chapter 5 Resources:
Brown, Gail. *Sensational Silk.* Portland, Oregon: Palmer-Pletsch Associates, 1982. 126 pages. Thorough book on sewing with silk and silk-like synthetics. It includes an explanation of the manufacturing processes, types of silk, and how to preshrink silk so that it can be washed. Available at fabric stores.

Brown, Gail, and Karen Dillon. *Sew a Beautiful Wedding.* Portland, Oregon: Palmer-Pletsch Associates, 1980. 127 pp. Available in most fabric stores. Good reference for selecting a flattering pattern, fitting and sewing the dress for those who choose a traditional wedding gown. Has convertibility suggestions to make a traditional dress wearable again, and a good, short section on "Recycling An Antique Wedding Dress or Fabric," complete with a recipe for dying new fabric (with tea!) to match slightly darkened or yellowed heirloom fabric.

FOLKWEAR, The Taunton Press, 63 S. Main Street, P. O. Box 5506, Newtown, CT 06470-5506. An unusual assortment of ethnic and historic patterns for men, women, and children (most for women), including a pattern for an Edwardian bridal gown. Look for their retail-sized pattern catalog in some sewing stores.

Harper House, P.O. Box 400, Gratz, PA 17030-0440; telephone (717) 365-3381. Catalog $5.; Reproduced antique patterns, very authentic.

McCormick, Terry. *The Consumer's Guide to Vintage Clothing*, New York: Dembner Books, 1987. 248 pp. Comprehensive guide to shopping for vintage clothes: how to tell the difference between a tear and fabric disintegration, fitting differences, mending and restoration, fabric content and durability, cleaning and stains, etc. It also has an appendix with lists of sources for vintage patterns, vintage clothing shops throughout the country, sources for vintage clothing by mail, good technical and practical advice on storing your heirloom clothes.

The Natural Choice, Eco Design Co., 1365 Rufina Circle, Santa Fe, NM 87501. (505) 438-3448. Catalog source of clothing, household, personal care, and stationery items, among other things.

Ocarina Textiles, 16 Cliff St., New London, CT 06320; phone (203) 437-8189. Makes fabrics with FoxFibre™ organically grown, colored cotton. Herringbone and chevron patterns of two-tone, naturally colored cotton. Also sells tagua nut buttons, and buttons of other natural materials.

The Ohio Hempery, Inc., 7002 State Route 329, Guysville, OH 45735; phone 1-800-BUY HEMP (that's 1-800-289-4367) or (614) 662-4367. Their hemp fabrics and hemp/natural fiber blends are organically grown, and very fine quality (you should see the hemp-silk blend fabric).

Pierce, Margaret. *Heirloom Sewing* (4 books: I-IV cover various techniques from beginning to advanced). Margaret Pierce Inc., P. O. Box 4542, Dept. SB, Greensboro, NC 27404; phone (919) 292-6430. Catalog available for $2.; phone to check on current catalog price.

Pullen, Martha. *Heirloom Sewing for Women.*
Pullen, Martha. *Antique Clothing French Sewing.*
For either book, contact Martha Pullen Co., Inc., 518 Madison Street, Huntsville, AL 35801-4286; phone 1-800-547-4176 or (205) 533-9586.

Zieman, Nancy. *Sewing With Nancy.* Has a chapter entitled "Sew An Heirloom," with basic techniques. A good book for ordinary mortals to start with. Oxmoor House, Inc., Book Division of Southern Progress Corp., P.O. Box 2436, Birmingham, Alabama 35201.

Chapter 6: Decorations, Flowers

Decorations

Besides flowers, the greenest decorations you can probably find are live, rented greenery. Live plants filter the air of various toxins; different plants seem to specialize in reducing or removing different substances. See Chapter 7 under Gifts for a list of plants that have been determined to be effective at filtering the air. The telephone book classifieds in my area list "Plants —Interior Design, Leasing & Maintenance." Both of the companies listed (o.k., so we're not a big city) also appear under "Plants-Retail." You can also check with nurseries or florists for leads.

Balloons and Streamers

Please don't use balloons, especially ones filled with helium! Helium-filled balloons often escape, drift for miles, and burst in a wilderness area, creating an eyesore and a hazard to wild animals who may eat and choke on them. If you feel you must use balloons with signs to your wedding/reception site, please arrange for someone to return to take down all the signs and balloons afterwards.

An alternative to balloons or conventional crepe paper streamers is paper streamers made from recycled paper. There are good, simple illustrated instructions for homemade paper streamers in *The Tightwad Gazette* by Amy Dacyzyn. You can be much more creative this way—crepe paper only comes in so many colors compared to recycled paper. Use colors that coordinate with your wedding, or combine several to create a rainbow effect—and recycle them when you're done.

Flowers

Flowers are the ultimate in green wedding decorations, especially if you do them yourselves, or have friends or relatives do them to your specifications. Here are some things to keep in mind:

• Use organically-grown flowers where you can.

• Use locally-grown flowers to cut down on transportation and air pollution. Try a farmer's market to find out about local sources of flowers.

• Use in-season flowers. These avoid energy-intensive winter greenhousing, for instance, or long-distance transportation. For example, lilacs out of season are available through florists, but must be flown in from Holland or France.

• Choose alternatives to disposable floral mechanics such as floral foam or wire.

• Compost all floral scraps—and corsages, boutonnieres, and bouquets, if their recipients are not going to preserve them.

• Preserve flowers naturally, without silica gel or other overpackaged materials.

A garden wedding

One way to save money on wedding flowers is to get married outdoors in a flower garden or other natural setting, and use the natural beauty of the site in lieu of floral arrangements. A local flower garden near my home also is an educational site for organic gardening methods. Small signs draw visitors' attention to gardening techniques used there in place of chemical pesticides or fertilizers. The flowers are lovely, and there is a large bush with showy, fragrant white flowers that grows in a natural arch—perfect for the ceremony and wedding photos. With such lovely surroundings, no other decoration is needed.

Organically grown flowers

If you decide to have cut flowers, using organically grown flowers is a good way to support sustainable agriculture. Also, you can save quite a bit of money by arranging your own flowers. Finding blooms that are grown without chemical pesticides or fertilizers can be as easy as using flowers from your own garden. Plant flowers that keep well, such as roses, daisies statice, gladioluses, carnations or pinks. If you don't have a garden and don't have the time or space to start one now, a local food co-op, produce stand, health food store or nursery is a good place to inquire about sources for organically grown flowers. Unless you grow them yourself (see **Wildflowers** below), leave wildflowers where they belong—in the wild, where they can reseed for the future.

Edible flowers

An extension of using organically grown flowers is to grow your own edible flowers organically. You can use edible flowers as boutonnieres, arrangements, bouquets, and even cake decorations. See the Cake Decorations section in Chapter 8 for more on edible flowers.

Wildflowers

The way to use wildflowers in your wedding without disrupting wildlife habitat is to grow them yourself, on land you are helping to restore to a wild state. In *Landscaping With Wildflowers*, Jim Wilson thoroughly describes how to garden with native wildflowers. The book is divided into regions, with hints on how to select what to grow, lots of beautiful color photos of the flowers, and addresses for obtaining seeds. Gardening with native plants is beneficial to wildlife, saves water, and promotes plant biodiversity. Not everyone has the space—or time—to grow wildflowers for their own wedding, but if you do, this book is a valuable resource. See the Bibliography for publisher information.

Reusable, useful floral mechanics

For your flowers, choose quality components that can have other uses once your wedding is over. For corsages and boutonnieres, try posy holders. For bouquets, make a nosegay, presentation bouquet, or simply put flowers in a basket. Rent or borrow good vases rather than buying cheap plastic ones. Instead of chunks of floral foam (called Oasis), position flowers in vases with a thick layer of smooth pebbles on the vase bottom. Use cornstarch clay to position flowers in baskets (see Appendix for recipe). For nosegays and other bouquets and floral items, choose good quality satin, grosgrain or French silk ribbon, not the cheap gift wrap type that frays on the edges. That way the ribbon can have a second life as hair ribbons, part of gift wrap, in crafts or school art projects, or trim or accents on clothing. Avoid floral wire and tape, plastic bouquet hol-ders with foam, excess yards of cheap ribbon, and the artificial toss bouquet.

Before you start

If you purchase cut flowers, pick them up the afternoon of the day before your wedding. Store them in water, covered loosely with a (recycled!) plastic bag in your fruit-free refrigerator. Your fridge needs to be free of fruit because ripening fruit, especially apples, gives off gasses that wilt fresh cut flowers. Before arranging, cut the stems on the diagonal under water, so that tiny air bub-bles don't form to block the passage of water up the stem's circulatory system. There are all sorts of ways to condition flowers before arranging—and they vary widely with the flower type. If you're really serious about it (and I have to admit I'm not, which is why the roses in my wedding bouquet were all half-opened—I liked them that way), figure out which flowers you'll be using, and read Jo Packham's, Malcolm Hillier's or Jane Packer's books on flower arranging listed in the Bibliography.

Corsage and boutonniere alternatives

Conventional corsages are wrapped in floral tape, may be wired, and often have a cheap faux pearl stick pin for attaching them to clothes. I always keep my stick pins, but still, most people are eventually going to throw most of that in the trash. The compost bin won't digest floral tape. Try posy holders instead, and compost the flowers.

• **Posy holders** are a nondisposable alternative to corsages. They make nice gifts, too. A posy holder is a stick pin attached to a small glass or silver tube that can hold a few fresh flowers, and sometimes a bit of water. They were popular adornments for women of the nineteenth century. You may be fortunate enough to find an affordable one at an antique shop. Here are three non-antique sources.

• A sterling silver reproduction in at least two styles is available from **Hand & Hammer** Silversmiths, 2610 Morse Lane, Woodbridge, VA 22192; 1-800-SILVERY.

• For good, reasonably-priced handblown glass posy holders, contact **The Dragon's Lair**, 1215 Harris, # 3, Bellingham, WA 98225 (360) 738-1242. They do custom work.

• Another source of glass posy holders is **Two's Company**, which only sells wholesale, so their address and number are not included here. Look in florists' and gift shops for other items of theirs, identified by packaging with their name, or ask the manager if the store carries any of their merchandise. Posy holders are a seasonal item, so ask well in advance of spring/summer. If you can't find them in local gift stores, check with Holly Mayshark, owner of **Holly's Fine Flowers**, 825 Water Street, Port Townsend, WA 98368; (206) 385-5428. She orders posy holders, although not in infinite quantities, so plan ahead. She usually first gets them in around December, and has them for the spring and summer. Tell her you read about her in *Green Weddings*.

• If the posy holder doesn't appeal to you, and your attendants are the type of people who reuse things like cheap faux pearl stick pins, make tiny nosegays out of a single blossom and some greenery, tie with narrow good quality satin ribbon, and pin with the stick pin. Save the ribbon and pin, and compost the blossom and greenery. Not ideal, but someone who does crafts may have a use for those leftover ribbons and pins.

Bouquets
• Nosegay
This is simply a bunch of flowers tied with ribbon. It can be very effective and lovely. Put flowers with fragile stems on the inside of the nosegay, and those with tougher stems on the outer edge next to the ribbon. That way, stems that could bleed or shred are protected from being crushed. Give the stems of the nosegay a gentle twist so that they spiral and make the flowers spread out. Very branchy flowers like baby's breath work nicely if you tightly rubber-band all the stems together and cover the rubber band with a ribbon. Make nosegays the morning of the wedding since

they will have no water source, and stand them in ice water when they are not being held.

• **Basket with flowers**

This is simple—so simple that no one thinks of it. There are many opportunities for creativity—and reycling—with baskets. The baskets can be purchased second hand, be reused, or both. They can double as table decorations at the reception. The bride can have an elaborate, beribboned one if desired, the attendants simpler ones. To arrange cut flowers without throwaway materials, consider laying flowers in oval flat baskets with two open ends instead of rounded sides. Another option is to make cornstarch clay (see Appendix). A lump of it can be put in a basket, and flowers inserted into it. If you use nontoxic flowers (carnations, roses, etc.—NOT daffodils, oleanders, delphiniums, etc.), you can tint the clay and give it to a child when you are finished with it. See the Cake Decorations section in Chapter 8 for more on edible flowers. Good quality wooden excelsior (long, narrow curlicued wood shavings, sometimes tinted) can provide structure for lightweight flowers such as baby's breath, or give short-stemmed flowers something to rest upon in deeper baskets. The excelsior can be reused in gift baskets—which is a good way to obtain it.

For another flower basket alternative, tuck potted flowers or flowering bedding plants into baskets. As with baskets of cut flowers, these "bouquets" can double as reception table decorations. Container edges can be camouflaged with excelsior, and plants can be used in the garden of your home, or given as gifts. Examples of choices are begonias, heather, impatiens, Johnny jump-ups, lobelia, pansies, primroses, petunias, star jasmine, sweet alyssum, or sweet William.

- **Single flower**

Carry a single flower such as a calla lily or rose, or place it in something you carry, such as a Bible or prayer book. Or the stem can be wrapped in French silk ribbon, which can of course be used again; select a flower that will not leak lots of plant juice and stain the ribbon. A calla lily can be dramatic, especially with clothes with very simple, elegant lines.

- **Presentation bouquet**

This is the bouquet that is often given to leading performers at the close of a final performance: leading actors on the last night of a play, prima ballerinas, soloists with the orchestra, etc. A large spray of about two dozen long stem roses of a single color are carried in the crook of one bent arm, and drape attractively over the arm just a bit. There may be a bit of greenery added— perhaps fern. This looks impressive, and it doesn't need to be limited to roses.

Fussless method: Start with about two dozen long stemmed flowers (single flowers per stem seem to work best). You can always use fewer flowers if the bouquet is too thick. Remove extra foliage—a few leaves are fine, but once the flowers are arranged, they'll be more like a shrub and less like a bouquet if every leaf is left on.

Arrange the flowers by laying the longer stemmed ones at the back or bottom of the bouquet, with the shortest ones on top. Stack them staggered to get the layered effect if they are all the same length. Leave stem ends as they are. You're done. Good luck, and don't drop it.

Fussy method: Trim the stems with a sharp knife, making a diagonal cut. Stick each stem end in a flower tube from a florist or craft/floral supply store—this means you end up with something extraneous that needs to be reused or given away. Better yet, skip the flower tubes and arrange as above. When flowers are arranged to your satisfaction, wrap them in a large square/rectangle of starched Battenburg lace or Irish linen, so that the lace forms a cone around the flowers, with the point of the open end at the center back of the bouquet. You'll want to experiment with this beforehand to see what size of fabric works best. For environmentally safe starch, put 1 tablespoon of cornstarch and a cup of cold water in a clean spray bottle and shake well. Spray and iron at the correct setting. Refrigerate; discard within a week.

- **Other ideas**

Be creative. You may find a carryable, attractive container suitable for wedding flowers that you would use again as a decoration in your home. Antique stores sometimes have "bride's baskets," medium-sized, flat-bottomed glass baskets in which flowers could be arranged, carried, and double as decoration. An art gallery that deals with glassblowers' work may have an interesting glass cornucopia or other unusual shape that could be filled with flowers and carried by the bride. Of course, only buy something that will have a second life beyond your wedding. These need to be items that you will use again, or can give as gifts to people who will genuinely appreciate them.

Organic flowers in winter

For organic flowers in winter months, you can either grow your own everlastings (see section below), or you can try forcing bulbs or branches from spring-blooming trees such as apple, peach, cherry, forsythia, etc. Since these types of flowers are a winter luxury, use them economically in simple ikebana style arrangements or sprays instead of profuse, summery types of bouquets. Or make them go further by combining them with everlastings; dried statice is especially vivid.

Most bulbs require cooling for many weeks before they can be forced. Several that do not require cooling are included in the tazetta division of the daffodil family:
• Paperwhite narcissus (*Narcissus tazetta 'Paperwhite Grandiflora'*—white)
• Grand Soleil d'Or narcissus (*Narcissus tazetta 'Grand Soleil d'Or'*—yellow)
• Chinese sacred lilies (*Narcissus tazetta orientalis*—white)
• 'Cragford' narcissus (*Narcissus tazetta 'Cragford'*—white petals, red "cup")
• 'Geranium' narcissus (*Narcissus tazetta 'Geranium'* —white petals, orange-red "cup")

Procedure for forcing bulbs

Fill an attractive, nondraining bowl with clean pebbles or washed gravel to within 1" of the top. Add water until it is nearly to the top of the pebbles or gravel. Place bulbs on top of pebbles, and cover the bottom third of each bulb with enough pebbles or gravel to anchor it in place. Keep the container in a cool, dark place for 2 to 3 weeks until the roots are well-established, and the bulbs have green shoots. Then bring them out into the light until they bloom, and at this point find a less well-lighted place to maintain the blooms. Throughout this process, keep the water level constant. You may want to tie a ribbon loosely around the stems after they reach 9"-10" or so to keep them from falling over. Somehow the homegrown forced bulbs never look quite as upright and tidy as the ones in gardening books. The whole process takes from 6 to 9 weeks. You can plant as early as mid-October, for late November to early December blooms.

For a continuous supply of blooms, gardeners recommend planting a new batch every two weeks. My advice is to spread out the plantings so that they bloom—you hope—over a three-week range around your wedding date.

These bulbs may be so exhausted after forcing that you may have to compost them. Otherwise, try planting the bulb and root in very well-fertilized soil in the spring when the weather has warmed up.

If you are serious about forcing some bulbs for wedding flowers and/or decorations, check one or two good books about bulbs out of the library. None of these flowers are edible.

Fedco Seeds, Inc. sell seeds and bulbs that are unfumigated. Their catalog costs $2. Fedco Seeds,

Inc., P.O. Box 520, Waterville, ME 04903; phone (207) 873-7333.

Forcing blossoms on branches

If you or an agreeable friend, neighbor or relative have forsythia or flowering fruit trees, these can be a source of organic winter flowers. Do not overprune the trees in your quest for blossoms; friends won't thank you if they have a significantly reduced crop of fruit, or a tree with no flowers in the spring. Use these winter blooms in simple, ikebana style arrangements. If you plan to use them in bouquets, make a simple presentation bouquet for the bride and small individual sprays for attendants. Boutonnieres and corsages could be one or two single blooms with a tiny bit of evergreen foliage.

Procedure for forcing blooms on branches

When the very smallest of buds have formed (usually sometime in November), cut unsprayed branches from one or a combination of the following trees: red hawthorn, redbud (Judas Tree; *Cercis canadensis* or *Cercis siliquastrum*), apple, peach, cherry, pear, flowering quince, plum, apricot, almond, forsythia. **Note:** of these flowers, only apple and redbud are edible. In her book *Edible Flowers* , Cathy Wilkinson Barash warns readers to eat apple flowers in moderation because they may contain cyanide precursors (like the seeds do).

Soften the bottom 2 1/2 to 3" of each stem by hammering it several times. This helps the branch to absorb water.

Place branches in a large glass jar or vase of water, keeping all buds and leaves above the surface of the water. Remove leaves and buds from the bottom of the branch, if necessary. Don't mix the types in the jar; if you have more than one type of flower, group each type in its own separate jar.

Keep the jar(s) in a dark place until the buds have grown large, about six weeks or so. During this process, as the water evaporates, add more cool water. Once the buds are large, bring the jars out into a well-lit room or near a window (if you live someplace that gets winter sun). The procedure takes about 7 weeks. The length of time for blooming to occur will vary, so you may want to be on the safe side and take a few branches out into the light at 4 or 5 day intervals instead of all at once, just to make sure you have fresh blooms in time for your wedding.

Bouquet preservation

If you compost your bouquet once it fades, there's just one less thing being saved to become someone else's junk seventy years later. However, if you decide you must keep your bouquet, use simple, natural methods to preserve it. Avoid using silicon crystals and other materials that create a need for more equipment, and come in packaging that must be disposed of somehow.

The easiest way to preserve your bouquet naturally is by choosing flowers that are everlastings, such as statice, roses in bud form, or baby's breath.

Another option is to have your bouquet made of dried flowers (very Victorian), so it is already preserved. To preserve fresh flowers, simply tie the bunch with cotton string or secure with a rubber band and hang upside down to dry. This is important for roses, which will dry out in a drooped position if not hung upside down. Colors may not be as intense as with a silicone preservative, but the simplicity of the process is worth it.

Again, compost any bouquets or arrangements you don't preserve. For nosegays, simply compost the flowers and save the ribbon for reuse.

Everlastings you can grow and dry yourself
The flowers on the following two pages are everlastings, which means that they can be preserved. Only everlastings that can be air dried are listed. These are not edible; even edible flowers such as roses will become dusty, so don't eat them. For a Victorian style wedding, roses, statice and baby's breath would work very nicely.

Pearly everlasting and tansy are listed, even though they may not be everyone's idea of wedding flowers, because they preserve so well. Also, some people like wildflowers for a wedding, and these two are common enough that they can be picked.

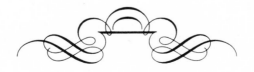

common name (scientific name)	color(s)
baby's breath (Gypsophila paniculata, G. elegans)	white, pink
delphinium (Delphinium grandiflorum, D. elatum)	blue/purple/white; pink/red/yellow
larkspur (Consolida ambigua, C. orientalis, C. regalis)	blue, pink, white
pearly everlasting (Anaphalis margaritacea)	off-white
rose (Rosa)	virtually all
statice (Limonium sinuatum)	white, purple, pink
tansy (Tanacetum vulgare)	yellow

season	comments
summer	hang to dry; very branchy
late spring to early fall	hang to dry; or dry standing in a dry vase or jar
spring to summer	hang to dry or dry standing in a dry vase when half of flowers are fully opened
late summer	hang in bunches to dry; common wildflower/weed
early to late summer	closed buds dry best; hang down to dry
summer	hang upside down or stand stems upright to dry
summer	hang in bunches to dry; common wildflower/weed

To hang flowers to dry, first remove any foliage you don't want. Generally, the quicker flowers dry, the better their color is preserved, and there is less possibility of mold or mildew. Excess foliage slows down the drying process. Once the extra foliage is removed, gather loose bunches of flowers, tie with cotton string or secure stems with a rubber band, and hang upside down to dry. Make sure the blooms are not crowded, so that the process isn't slowed down. The place where you hang them should be well-ventilated, warm and dry. Once the flowers are dried, store in a sealed paper bag or box away from dust, dampness, and strong light when they are not part of an arrangement.

Chapter 7: Music, Photography, and Gifts

Music

For both your ceremony and reception, consider "unplugged" music or minimal use of electricity. A good musician or ensemble is well worth the investment. Ceremony choices could include one or more of the following: organ or piano, harp, string quartet, classical guitar, brass choir, solo flute, *a cappella* or accompanied vocal ensemble, recorder consort—as you can see, the possibilities for live, suitable music are many.

For the reception, you could have any of the above (except organ), jazz or classical piano, a roving violinist, even a band that plays big band swing. None of those require electricity, except the organ, and the swing band leader.

To find musicians who perform at weddings, check local bridal shops for names and phone numbers of musicians. Other sources to check include conservatories or the music department of a local university; and music stores, which may keep lists of wedding musicians or a bulletin board with their business cards. To locate a band, check with the local Musicians' Union.

Some churches don't allow dancing, but have lovely reception facilities. If you're looking at a reception location that can accommodate live music but does not allow dancing, the food/ conversation/music reception without band, disc jockey or emcee will work in such a location. And you're arranging for use of less electricity, with no transportation between ceremony and reception.

One last word on music. Be sure to include musicians in the head count for the meal, if there is one. Feed them. They deserve it.

Photography

Some bridal magazines have advertisements for disposable cameras (choice of colors, with your names and wedding date embossed in silver or gold—minimum order 100) to be distributed at your reception, for guests to take candid shots of one another. This is wasteful. If you really like the idea of guests snapping one another's photos, instruct friends and family to bring their cameras from home; you can supply them with film, if you like.

Since photo processing involves toxic chemicals, you may want to consider limiting the number of pictures your photographer takes. A skilled photographer can take a good selection of posed and candid shots without using excessive amounts of film. An interesting alternative to lots of photographs is to take fewer pictures, and hire an artist to do sketches during the ceremony and/or reception, or a portrait beforehand. For various artists' supplies, see *Nontoxic, Natural, and Earthwise*.

For displaying wedding photos, you'll want to take frames and photo albums into consideration.

The demand for frames and other items made of rare tropical hardwoods such as rosewood, teak and mahogany spells depletion of those resources in tropical countries worldwide. Alternatives include purchasing secondhand frames from antique shops and secondhand stores, or using frames of alternative materials. Unique and interesting alternative materials range from recycled timbers from demolished turn-of-the-century homes to woven pandam leaves. For photo albums, check Earth Care, The Natural Choice and Seventh Generation catalogs from time to time. To make your own photo album, see Flora Fennimore's *The Art of the Handmade Book* (mentioned in the Guest Book section of Chapter 9 of this book).

Gifts : Giving

For items that range from T-shirts to housewares, and are sold by charitable nonprofit groups, see *Gifts That Make a Difference,* and *Gifts That Save the Animals,* both by Ellen Berry. Foxglove Publishing, 598 David Pkwy., Dayton, OH 45429; phone (513) 293-5649.

attendants' gifts

Consider giving subscriptions to environmental magazines, or a membership in The Nature Conservancy.

Adults
• *Audubon*, The Magazine of the National Audubon Society, National Audubon Society, 950 3rd Avenue, New York, NY 10022-2705.

• *E Magazine.* Earth Action Network, Inc., 28 Knight Street, Norwalk, CT 06851; (203) 854-5559.
• The Nature Conservancy, 1815 North Lynn Street, Arlington, VA 22209; (703) 841-5300.

Children
• The *Dolphin Log,* The Cousteau Society, 8440 Santa Monica Blvd., Los Angeles, CA 90069-4221.
• Owl *Magazine, The Discovery Magazine for Children,* The Young Naturalist Foundation, 56 the Esplanada, Suite, 306, Toronto, Ontario, M5E 1A7, Canada.
• *Ranger Rick,* National Wildlife Federation, 1400 16th St. NW, Washington, DC 20036.

Gifts: Receiving

Two green options for wedding gifts are: green gifts; or donations to charity. Let's look at each.

Green Gifts

The conventional (and convenient) way for guests to select wedding gifts that the bride and groom actually need or want is through a gift registry. The bridal couple goes to a particular department or housewares store, selects items they need, and the store makes the list available to any guest/patron. If you choose a gift registry, you might consider selecting one of the catalogs at the back of the book, such as Seventh Generation, The Natural Choice, Earth Care or Real Goods. Many of them, such as Seventh Generation, already have gift registry services. Earth, General store in

Brooklyn, New York, has an environmental bridal registry (the first, according to Will Nixon in the Nov./Dec. 1992 issue of *E Magazine*). They offer housewares such as recycled glassware and unbleached cotton bed linens, and wedding items such as photo albums of recycled paper. Earth General, 72 Seventh Avenue, Brooklyn, NY 11217; phone (718) 398-4648.

If you decide to register with a department store, select one that has products and business practices that benefit the environment. Look for things such as green cotton or organic cotton sheets and towels, and recycled content glassware. See *SHOPPING FOR A BETTER WORLD* for ratings of companies' products the department store may carry, or choose a company listed in the *National Green Pages.*

Besides organic cotton linens and recycled glass, green gifts could include a composter or a worm composting bin (see the Real Goods catalog), or house plants to filter indoor air. House plants are particularly nice to have if you're moving into a new apartment or house, complete with toxic fumes from paint, linoleum and vinyl carpet. The September 1987 issue of *Practical Homeowner* has an article by Becky Gillette about plants tested by a NASA scientist for their capacity to remove formaldehyde and benzene from the air. Here are the plants, listed in decreasing order of effectiveness, according to Dr. B. C. Wolverton. Their scientific names are listed first, followed by their common or commercial names, compiled with the help of the *Sunset New Western Garden Book.* According to Dr. Wolverton, you should use about 15 to 20 of these plants for a 1,800-square-foot house, optimally near air ducts and circulation vents. Generally, the larger the leaf surface, the more filtration capability.

1. Philodendron scandens oxycardium
    heart leaf philodendron
    or philodendron cordatum
2. Philodendron domesticum
    elephant ear philodendron
    or philodendron 'Hastatum'
3. Chlorophytum elatum
    green spider plant
4. Philodendron selloum
    lacy tree philodendron
    also variety 'Lundii'
5. Aloe vera
6. Scindapsus aereus
    golden pothos
7. Aglonema modestum
    Chinese evergreen
8. Brassaia arboricola
    mini-schefflera; Hawaiian elf schefflera
9. Peperomia obtusifolia
    peperomia
    variety 'Minima' has smaller leaves
10. Spathiphyllum 'clevelandii'
    peace lily
11. Dracaena fragrans 'massangeana'
    corn plant
12. Sanseveria trifasciata
    mother-in-law tongue; snake plant

Gillette's article also includes plans for a plant-based air filter devised by Dr. Wolverton.

Donations to Charity

Perhaps this is your second wedding, or you're marrying later in life and already have two households full of possessions. You decide you'd like to channel that giving impulse elsewhere. Gift-giving at weddings can be an emotionally charged issue. Some people, particularly older relatives, may feel that you are depriving them of an opportunity to express their love if they cannot give you a material present. Here are some options that may satisfy both you and them.

In lieu of gifts, have your guests donate to one of several charities. Compile a list of environmental and charitable organizations you would be happy to support. To get the word out to your guests:

1) print the list and a short explanation directly on the invitation*, or

2) print the list on a separate piece of paper, to be enclosed with the invitation* (if you're enclosing a map to get to the wedding/reception site, print the list on the reverse side), or

3) leave the list with friends and both sets of parents so that they can field inquiries about what you would like, or

4) include the charities' addresses on the registries of department and gift stores.

* NOTE: It is considered to be in poor taste to mention gifts on a wedding invitation. However, I have received at least one invitation that told

me where the couple was registered for gifts, and I found it very helpful. The following simple sentences are examples of wordings that convey the spirit of what you're trying to do:

"At this time of great joy for us, we cannot help remembering others less fortunate. In lieu of gifts to us, a fund has been set up in our name with the Housing Authority (Salvation Army, etc.) to help a homeless family." (Include address and account name). Or, "We are blessed to have everything we need. We would be honored by a donation to one of the following charities:" (Include a list of charities).

If you don't yet have a favorite environmental charity, see *50 Simple Things You Can Do to Save the Earth,* or *The Green Consumer* for a list of environmental organizations to get you started. *The Green Consumer* has a short narrative on each one. Before you decide upon a particular charity, do some research to make sure that you agree with its goals and achievements.

Another approach, as used in the sample invitation wording above, is to set up an account for donations directly through an organization. If a single organization is chosen—a local organization that will distribute the monies to a homeless family, for example—often the guests can feel that they are making a tangible contribution to a worthwhile cause.

Chapter 8: Food

Here are some guidelines to keep in mind as you research environmentally sound food choices for your reception:
• Use less meat or no meat at all.
• Reduce the amount of other animal products you consume—dairy products, eggs, fish—or omit them altogether.
• Purchase organically grown produce whenever possible. Better yet, grow your own vegetables and fruits organically.
• Purchase food items in bulk with your own containers, whenever possible.
• Eat only in-season fruits and vegetables.
• As much as possible, purchase and eat locally-grown foods over ones that need much transportation to get to you.
• Donate uneaten reception food to a local shelter for the homeless.
• Recycle all food cans and beverage bottles.

The Vegan Reception
Foods with animal proteins require more resources—land and water—than do vegetable proteins. And vegetable proteins and products, with the exception of vegetable oil, can all be safely composted. (Meat, bones, dairy products, and vegetable oil are noncompostable. They break

down too slowly.) A vegetarian reception is green. A vegan reception can be even greener. Even if you do not normally follow a vegan diet—which means avoidance of all animal products, including meat, poultry, and dairy products—you can have delicious vegan food at your wedding reception. Since you will be feeding many people, this is a great way to put green consumerism to work, especially if you purchase organically grown ingredients.

Organically grown produce gives the earth—the soil, water, plants, animals and us—a respite from the unremitting dose of agricultural chemicals used to control every aspect of the growing process. When we buy—or grow—organic, we are reducing the amount of pesticides that farmers, farm workers and their families will ingest, and the amount of pesticides that will be washed into the ocean or show up in our drinking water sources. It's a win-win situation.

In-season produce is vitally important. When we eat a seasonal fruit or vegetable fresh year-round, we are eating something that has been grown in another hemisphere. That means extensive transportation. It also means that because of our economic demand for this food, it is being planted instead of an indigenous fruit, vegetable or grain. Also, these wonder fruits and veggies, flown in from the ends of the globe, are probably more heavily dosed with pesticides and fungicides than if they didn't have to cross political and agricultural borders. Martin Teitel's *Rain Forest in Your Kitchen* has an excellent explanation of why in-season produce is vital to biodiversity, both here and far away.

Local, organically-grown, in-season ingredients are the best of all possible worlds. For its list of organic farmers and wholesaler (over 1,000 listed), updates on state and federal regulations, and list of Organic Certification Groups, the *National Organic Directory* is the most thorough of the resources listed here. With shipping and handling, it costs about $40. Contact the Community Alliance With Family Farmers (CAFF for short), P.O. Box 464, Davis, CA 95617; phone 1-800-852-3832. If you just want to find a good local natural food store with organic produce, first try the classified section of the phone book. Second, read *The Tofu Tollbooth* by Dar Williams. It has over 700 listings of natural foods stores that the reviewers judged to be of good quality, and a list of some of the amenities of each. With a few noted exceptions, most of the stores have organic produce. Also, see the *National Green Pages* for co-ops and food stores that carry organically grown food. Finally, be on the lookout for green news stories and read magazines such as *IN BUSINESS* to find out what green supermarkets there may be near you.

The Buffet

One way to handle food at your reception is to have a sit-down buffet. Guests can serve themselves, mingle, and visit with you, too. An even easier method is to have a stand-up reception with lots of made-ahead hors d'oeuvres set out buffet-style. *The Vegan Gourmet*, by

Susann Geishopf-Hadler and Mindy Toomay (Prima Publishing; see the bibliography for publisher's address) has tasty recipes for appetizers, salads, side dishes and entrees for special occasions. The recipes serve 4-6 people, so you would need to plan on increasing them.

Issue #2 July 1993 of *Veggie Life* has "A Wedding Day Buffet," an article by Lillian Kayte, with vegetarian recipes. Kayte includes preparation times, serving amounts, and a basic nutritional analysis of each recipe. Not all recipes are vegan, but some can be adapted. Delicious! Look for it at your library; all the back issues of it are sold out, according to the July 1995 issue.

Another excellent out-of-print resource is Evelyn Findlater's *The Natural Entertainer*. For our purposes, its best feature is a collection of recipes for an elegant wedding buffet for 50 guests. In addition to a Midsummer Celebration Menu or Wedding Feast, it also has recipes and menus for formal dinner parties, with recipes using ingredients available in each of the four seasons. This is vitally important from an environmental standpoint. With this book, you can plan an elegant vegetarian or vegan menu of in-season foods for any time of the year. For the wedding menu, she includes a list of tasks that can be done ahead of time, and a time-line for them. The main recipes are vegetarian, using dairy products and eggs, with adaptations for both vegans and meat-lovers. The recipes are delicious. The only disadvantage is that it is a British cookbook, and certain ingredients that we would measure out (in the U.S. and Canada) are weighed instead, such as nuts or sliced fruit.

If you can't find *The Natural Entertainer* in your local library, via interlibrary loan, or in a used bookstore near you, a bookstore which gets copies from time to time is Michael's Books, 109 Grand Avenue, Bellingham, WA 98225; (360) 733-6272. They're quite helpful.

If you want a simple homestyle vegan brunch, lunch or dinner reception for a large crowd, *Food Not Bombs* is a handy resource. *Food Not Bombs* is a social activism book (based upon the radical concept that there is enough food around to feed everyone), with recipes for simple vegan foods in large quantities, usually to serve 100. The authors state that their serving size is 6 to 7 ounces per serving of food; the recipes will need to be increased or the guest list decreased for larger servings. I would recommend this book to anyone planning a large "homemade" reception; there is no guesswork, since the quantities and preparation times are already figured out, and the recipes have been tried. If you're having friends help you, you can all get together and decide who wants to prepare what. Also, you can combine recipes from several of the categories. An ample wedding brunch would be a buffet with a fresh fruit platter or fruit salad, granola, muffins and breads, scrambled tofu, fried potatoes, one salad and one lunch/dinner dish. Add the cake and punch recipes in this chapter, and you're set.

For a reception that is midway between standard mealtimes, such as a brunch or an afternoon reception after lunchtime, try to use a few foods that will fit into either meal. For a brunch buffet, a fruit platter and filled crepes span both breakfast and lunch menus, and you can add breakfast and lunch items for a complete spread: granola, muffins, scrambled tofu and fried potatoes; and sandwich materials and a salad. Crepes are a good addition to any buffet. My favorite is wholewheat vegan crepes filled with duxelles and covered with a bechamel (white) sauce. *The New Laurel's Kitchen* has a delicious recipe for crepes made without eggs or dairy products (low cholesterol). The recipes for duxelles and a vegan bechamel sauce are given below. The sauce can be seasoned any number of ways, but to be honest, I prefer a real bechamel sauce made with milk.

Duxelle-stuffed Crepes with Béchamel Sauce— Procedure:

Fill each crepe with 2 heaping tablespoons of duxelles. Roll crepes up, placing seam-side down on an attractive heatproof serving platter. These stuffed crepes can be wrapped airtight, frozen and warmed up slowly in the oven (300 F), but they're best fresh. Another option is to make the crepes ahead of time and freeze them. Simply stack them, wrap edges tightly and freeze. Thaw at room temperature before separating.

Serve each crepe with a couple tablespoons of béchamel sauce.

Duxelles Fills 12-16 crepes

For this recipe, chop both the mushrooms and onions by hand. It makes a tremendous difference in the taste and texture. I like to have both mushrooms and onions mostly in tiny 1/8" to 1/16" pieces. Duxelles are very difficult to stop eating once you take a bite, so taste them sparingly!

    1 1/2 lb. mushrooms, very finely chopped
        (about 6-7 cups)
    1 1/2 medium onions, very finely chopped
        (about 1 1/2 cups)
    6 tablespoons soy margarine

Sauté onion in margarine over medium heat for about 2 minutes, stirring occasionally. Add mushrooms and turn heat to low. Continue cooking, stirring occasionally, until moisture is all absorbed and mushrooms are a coarse, shiny paste. If these have enough onion, they don't really need any other seasoning; otherwise add salt and pepper to taste. This is a good way to freeze mushrooms, and they can be made ahead of time and frozen until you make the crepes.

The following béchamel sauce is mild and can be seasoned with herbs to your taste. It is fine as it is for a sauce for the crepes, which are savory and complement it.

Vegan Béchamel (White) Sauce   makes 2 cups

6 tablespoons soy margarine
1/4 cup whole wheat pastry flour
1/2 teaspoon salt
1/4 teaspoon pepper
2 cups rice milk (Rice Dream works very well)

Melt the margarine over medium-low heat. Stir in the flour, salt and pepper, and slowly add the rice milk, stirring in a little at a time so that no lumps form. Bring to a boil, stirring constantly; lower heat. Cook for about 10 minutes over low heat so that raw flour taste is gone.

Beverages

For beverages also, try to use organically-grown products whenever possible. It is possible to have a perfectly nice reception with fruit punch, coffee, mineral water, and for toasting, a nonalcoholic sparkling juice such as apple cider, or any of the many other flavors that are available. Check *Nontoxic, Natural & Earthwise* under Juice in the chapter on food. An event does not have to feature alcohol to be special, and many venues charge extra if you will be serving alcohol at your event. Also, a nonalcoholic reception increases your options of reception sites; many churches have nice parish halls or reception rooms that are available if there is no alcohol involved in the reception.

For a list of organically-grown wines, or wines made without sulfites, see *Nontoxic, Natural, & Earthwise.*

When figuring out how much punch to serve, consider not only the number of guests, but the weather as well. Guests will be thirstier in hot weather.

According to a rental professional I spoke with, three gallons of punch is supposed to serve 100 people. This actually means that 96 people each have just one 4-ounce punch cup. That seems like an unreasonably small amount of punch, especially for a summer wedding. A more reasonable estimate is 20 servings per gallon. 100 guests would each get a little over 6 ounces of punch, which is much better.

Although the modest glass punchbowls you can purchase for home use generally hold 6 quarts comfortably with about 1 1/2" of extra space at the top, most punchbowls available at rental stores are sized by the gallon. I found various sizes of bowls in glass, stainless steel and silver. The standard sizes were 2, 3, 5 and 6 gallons. The larger sized bowls at the places I checked were in plastic (with a petal design) and stainless steel. The closer the bowl is to the 2 to 3-gallon size, the more potential there seems to be for a fancy design.

Since most punchbowl capacities are multiples of a gallon, the following basic recipe is for one gallon of punch, to be multiplied as needed. This recipe is intended as a starting point for your creativity. Vary it according to your own taste and what is available locally.

Basic Punch Formula—1 gallon

You'll notice that on a simple level, this recipe is half plain juice and half sparkling water. You can adjust the fizziness by substituting plain water for some of the sparkling mineral water, or vice versa.

2 12-ounce cans of frozen juice concentrate
2 quarts sparkling mineral water
1 cup water
1 quart juice (reconstituted, not in concentrate form)

Thaw the frozen concentrate in the refrigerator overnight, and chill remaining ingredients. Combine and serve. See optional garnishes below.

For a very light colored punch, use white grape juice concentrate or (filtered) apple juice concentrate, and other pale juices such as grapefruit.

Punch bowl garnishes

• Float fresh strawberry slices, mint leaves, fresh blueberries in the punch; choose fruits that will complement the color and flavor of the punch.

• Freeze water or fruit juice in unusual shapes, or freeze a piece of fruit or a small edible flower or in the center of each cube. For unusual shapes, fill the indentations in a high quality polyethylene candy mold 3/4 full of liquid. These type of molds are used for melted chocolate. If you purchase any, get double use out of them by using them first to make individual tofu chocolate candies as wedding favors. My favorite shapes are seashells such as scallops.

• Float a frozen juice or ice ring with flowers and mint leaves or carved fruit in the punchbowl. For a plain ice ring, use chilled distilled water; it will be less cloudy when it freezes.

In a ring mold, place sturdy edible flowers with stems removed, such as tiny spray roses, sweetheart roses, lavender, lilac, mint or basil flowers (African blue basil has lovely purple little flowers) and mint leaves. See the section on edible flowers under Cake Decorations, later in this chapter, or for a more complete list, *Edible Flowers: From Garden to Palate* by Cathy Wilkinson Barash. Add just enough distilled water or juice to cover flowers. Freeze; then add enough juice or water to fill ring 3/4 full. Freeze again, and keep in freezer until ready to add to the punch. To free the frozen juice from the ring mold, place ring mold in a shallow pan of warm water. Invert ring mold over punch bowl and ease ring into the punch; it will be about half submerged.

The Cake

Traditional wedding cake in North America seems to be white, yellow, or chocolate butter cake lavishly covered with buttercream. It is often tiered using throwaway plastic columns. Depending on the area of the country where the wedding takes place, there may be a cake top on the uppermost tier—anything from handblown glass to elaborate icing flowers to plastic wedding bells, or even that tiny plastic wedding couple standing on the top of the cake. There are several ways in which you can have a cake that is "greener" than the standard wedding cake:

1. Bake a cake yourself using eggs from organically-fed free-range chickens (or ones in large pens instead of cages), and dairy products from a small family-type farm where the animals are fed organic feed and no hormones. Anyone considering baking a wedding cake with dairy products and eggs needs Rose Levy Beranbaum's *The Cake Bible*. It is a wonderful resource for baking cakes of any size, and any recipe you bake will taste wonderful.

2. If you like option 1 above, but want a cake recipe without the entire cookbook, there is a recipe for Strawberry and Lemon Cream-Filled Butter Cake with White Chocolate Buttercream in the Thursday June 23, 1994 edition of *The Christian Science Monitor* ("Taking a Vow to Make Tasty Wedding Cakes," by Elizabeth Levitan Spaid).

3. One step better, in my opinion, is to bake and decorate a cake without any animal products. There are several vegan wedding cake recipes in this chapter.

4. Use finely ground whole wheat flour instead of bleached cake flour. When wheat kernels are milled into several products (wheat germ, unbleached flour, etc.) instead of just one, more packaging is created for the same amount of wheat than if it had all been ground into just whole wheat flour. And since you're getting all

the grain and its nutrients, whole wheat flour is less wasteful, nutritionally speaking.

5.   Use an alternative sweetener other than refined white or brown sugar.

6.   Forget about the cake top and use fresh edible flowers instead.   Or use fresh, not-so-edible flowers, and make sure they are in a container so that they do not touch the cake or icing. A small, shallow clean glass dish from a second hand shop is the type of thing that works well.

7.   Stack the cake tiers directly one on top of the other instead of using the unstable plastic Grecian-style columns that are so commonly used. Use wooden dowels, and save them (after the cake is cut) to give to someone who does crafts or makes wooden toys.   Again, Rose Levy Berenbaum's book is very helpful with instructions on tiering a cake (stacking the layers directly on top of one another without plastic columns).

8.   Instead of lots of piped icing decorations, consider using fresh edible flowers.

9. If you don't want to use an electric mixer, use a hand-cranked egg beater, or beat about 150 vigorous strokes by hand with a wooden spoon for each minute of electric mixer beating.

Alternative   sweeteners

White sugar is highly refined, and uses lots of water in the growing and processing— about 1 ton of water to produce 1 pound of sugar. It is not an energy-efficient process. Also, sugar grown in Florida may be grown on filled-in land in the Everglades, making it a poor choice of sweetener, environmentally speaking. Vegetarians may be interested to know that at some point in the refining process, sugar is passed through a column of hot coals that may consist of beef bone char. Chemicals are also used to obtain the white color. Sugar harvesting is also responsible for air pollution in parts of Hawaii. After all the sugar cane is harvested from a field, the field is then burned to drive away the rats that like to take refuge in cane fields. Virtually any time you see a huge, foul cloud of black smoke over there, that's what it is. Finally, I'll never forget a high school field trip I once took. Our destination was across the highway from a sugar refinery. The air smelled terrible! Perhaps it wasn't only the sugar, but I'll always associate that pollution with sugar production.

Of all the sweeteners, **honey** is the most natural and least refined, if strained and unpasteurized. The ideal is to find locally-grown honey from bees that pollinate organic crops or flowers, and are not treated with antibiotics. Vegans do not use honey, because it is an animal product. Here I differ from veganism, because I think that honey is the most environmentally benign of any of the sweeteners. It can be organically produced, be virtually unprocessed and unrefined, come from a very local source, and optimally is packaged only in glass with a reusable metal screw top lid—both of which recycle.

Sucanat is the brand name for evaporated, unrefined juice from sugar cane. It tastes similar to brown sugar, only richer. The consistency is closer to that of white sugar that has been exposed to moisture and has clumped slightly. Check with a food co-op or health food store.

Brown rice syrup makes a satisfactory vegan substitute for honey in frosting. It is moderately sweet, and has a pleasant, grainy taste. Again, chack with a food co-op or health food store.

Apple juice concentrate, when used in combination with ground or finely chopped dried fruits, is also a good natural sweetener. For delicious recipes, see *Naturally Sweet: Desserts Sweetened with Fruit* by Fran Raboff and Lynn Bassler (The Crossing Press, 97 Hanger Way, Watsonville, CA 95019).

A Vegan Wedding Cake: Basic Principles

To convert a standard cake recipe to vegan, substitute water or soy milk for regular milk (3 T. soy milk flour or defatted soy flour and 1 c.+ 1 T. water), and non-dairy soy margarine for butter. Tastewise, I would recommend water first, commercially-prepared soy milk next, and the soy flour-water mixture last. If whole eggs are only used as a binder, and not a leavening, you can simply omit them (this yields the best taste), or substitute 1 tablespoon soy flour and 1 1/2 tablespoon water for each egg. Eggs are used as leavening in any recipe where eggs and air are featured. If the recipe has no baking powder or soda, has stiffly beaten egg whites, or eggs that are beaten over hot water (as in a chiffon cake), the soy flour substitute will not work.

Don't be too surprised if the cake is slightly coarser, drier and has less height that a cake with eggs. Whatever you do, though, do not use brown rice syrup as a substitute for honey in a cake—or you'll have that cake around for a long, long time. Brown rice syrup gives cake a strangely gummy texture.

Here are recipes for four "environmentally-friendly" wedding cakes. I would urge you to halve the recipe and try your choice beforehand as a two-layer 9-inch cake with some leftover muffins, (or as an 8" square pan of Matrimonial Cake) so you can taste-test it. And if you don't like these recipes, see *Recipes from an Ecological Kitchen* by Lorna J. Sass, and try multiplying her recipe for Lemon Poppy Seed Cake, or Devil's Food Carob Cake.

Basic Cake Pan Preparations:
- Prepare three cake pans: a 6", 9" and 12," each 1 1/2" or 2" deep.
- Butter the inside of each pan with soy margarine, and flour it. You will be using each pan **twice**.
- Wrap the sides of each pan with a strip of aluminum foil in the following manner: Fold a strip of aluminum foil 1 1/2" wide, and wrap it around the side of the cake pan. Secure it with a straight pin (nail-type or glass head only; plastic may melt or give off fumes). Do this with each layer before baking it in the oven. It helps the layers bake evenly so that they stack flat for tiering, and will reduce the amount of cake you have to trim to make the layers level.

Vegan Spice Wedding Cake with Sucanat

7 3/4 cups fine whole wheat flour
3 tablespoons baking powder
1 1/2 teaspoons salt
2 teaspoons cinnamon
1 teaspoon nutmeg
1 teaspoon allspice
3 cups Sucanat
1 1/2 cups flavorless vegetable oil such as
    safflower or sunflower
3 cups water
2 tablespoons vanilla

Preheat oven to 350 degrees F. Prepare pans (see Basic Cake Pan Preparations above). Sift dry ingredients together, or mix on low for 1 minute with electric mixer to aerate. Add the vanilla and half of the oil and water, beating until well blended, about 1 minute. You may prefer to beat this with a wooden spoon, as batter will be thick and tends to crawl up the beaters; add small amount of water if needed. Scrape batter from sides of bowl to incorporate any unmixed flour. Add remaining liquid; beat another minute. Divide batter between the three pans—6", 9", and 12"—filling each about two thirds full. Bake small layer 25-35 minutes; medium layer 35-40 minutes; and 12" layer 35-45 minutes, or until layers test done with a toothpick or a piece of uncooked spaghetti. Cool pans on racks 10-15 minutes; invert onto plates and then back onto cooling racks without the pans. Wash, dry, and prepare the pans again. Make the recipe a second time, fill pans and bake. You will have two layers for each tier.

Vegan Carrot Spice Cake

This carrot cake is the perfect consistency for tiering. Some people find it a bit dry for a carrot cake, but a very moist cake will collapse under its own weight when tiered. Cover with "cream cheese" frosting (below); you may further decorate it with fresh edible flowers if you wish. Vegans may substitute 3 1/2 cups Sucanat for the 2 cups honey, and increase the water to 2 1/2 cups.

You will need to make the following recipe **twice**:
6 cups fine whole wheat flour
3 1/2 tablespoons baking powder
1 1/2 teaspoon salt
1 tablespoon cinnamon
1 1/2 teaspoons nutmeg
1 1/2 teaspoons allspice
2 tablespoons vanilla, optional
2 cups light honey
1 3/4 cups safflower oil
4 cups finely grated carrots
1 1/2 cups water
1 cup chopped walnuts
1 cup chopped raisins

Preheat oven to 350 degrees F. Prepare pans (see Basic Cake Pan Preparations above). Sift dry ingredients together, or mix on low for 1 minute with electric mixer to aerate. Add the vanilla and half of the honey, oil and water, beating until well blended. Add remaining liquid; beat. You may prefer to beat this with a wooden spoon, as batter will be thick and tends to crawl up the beaters; add small amount of water if needed. Stir in raisins, carrots and chopped walnuts. Divide batter between the three pans—6", 9", and 12"—filling each about two thirds full. Bake small layer 25-35 minutes; medium layer 35-40 minutes; and 12" layer 35-45 minutes, or until layers test done with a toothpick. Cool pans on racks 10-15 minutes; invert onto plates and then back onto cooling racks without the pans. Wash, dry, and prepare the pans again. Make the recipe a second time, fill pans and bake. You will have two layers for each tier.

Boiled Fruitcake: For the 4 cups of finely grated carrots, substitute 4 cups mixed dried fruit: figs, apricots, prunes, currants, cherries—your favorite combination. Sharp kitchen shears are a help in cutting up the dried fruit. Put dried fruit in a heavy-bottomed saucepan, add 2 cups of water, cover and simmer until fruit is tender, about 20 minutes. Add more water during cooking if fruit beings to stick to saucepan. Cool and mix batter as for Vegan Carrot Spice Cake above, adding boiled fruit in place of carrots. (Don't forget the chopped raisins and walnuts). Bake as for Vegan Carrot Spice Cake. This tastes very rich and brown-sugary with the substitution of 3 cups of Sucanat for the honey. Dark fruitcake was once the wedding cake of choice, and is still considered traditional today in England and Canada.

Unfrosted, this fruitcake makes a great breakfast bread.

For the more adventurous couple, there is Matrimonial Cake, known today in Canada as a snack cake. It seems to find its way mostly into Canadian home economics cookbooks, probably because it is easy to make. Matrimonial cake apparently originated in England, and was mentioned in writings in 1890 as traditional wedding fare in the counties of Yorkshire, Kent and Devon. It traditionally was round, and had a layer of currants sandwiched between a pastry top and bottom; the top was covered in sugar. Today it's really more of a date square. Since most people like this cake, you will probably need to make plenty. For round cakes, bake in springform pans. The pan sides can be removed, and the cakes can be set on attractive serving platters and surrounded by edible flowers before cutting. You can make extra rectangular cakes (in your old, grease-stained pans that you don't want anyone to see) in reserve for when the round cakes run out.

Matrimonial Cake

>   2 cups chopped dates
>   2/3 cup water
>   2 teaspoons lemon juice
>   2 cups uncooked oatmeal
>   2 cups whole wheat pastry flour
>   3/4 cup Sucanat
>   1 cup soy margarine
>   1 teaspoon vanilla

Preheat oven to 350 degrees F. Cook the dates, water and lemon juice over low heat until mixture is the consistency of a smooth paste and the water is blended in, up to 20 minutes. Cream the margarine and Sucanat; add vanilla. Add flour and oatmeal, and blend together to form crumbs. Pat half the crumbly mixture into an ungreased 9" x 13" pan. Spread with all of the date filling, and top with the remaining crumbs. Bake 20-30 minutes; do not brown. Cool and cut into squares. This cake is plain-looking but tasty, keeps well, and you don't have to fuss with frosting.

And finally, for those who want something really unique and wholesome, there is a rich, dark, uncooked wedding cake made of dried fruit, nuts, and roasted carob powder. Honey or rice syrup acts as a binder. The carob powder adds flavor and thickening. Vary the mix of dried fruit to suit your taste. Cut this cake in thin wedges using a sharp knife dipped in hot water between cuts. You can press it into a variety of shapes; you're not limited by cake pans. Try a 2" to 3" thick heart or flower-shaped cake. Frost with "cream cheese" frosting, or cover it with a 1/4" thick layer of marzipan pressed directly onto the cake (the "cream cheese" will undoubtedly look better), and strategically place edible flowers to cover flaws.

114

Carob Nut Fruitcake   enough for one 6" layer

  3 cups dried mission figs, cut into pieces (about
        1 lb.)
  1 cup raisins
  2/3 cup apricots, cut into pieces (about 1/4 lb.)
  3/4 cup cashew pieces or whole almonds
  enough honey or brown rice syrup to act as a
        binder—1 to 2 tablespoons
  2 tsp. vanilla, optional (gives the cake a rummy
        flavor—not everyone likes the taste)
  enough roasted carob powder to thicken, about
        1/4 to 1/2 cup

There are two methods to use to mix these
ingredients, depending on what equipment you
use.

Food Processor Method
    Cut up the figs and apricots with kitchen shears.
Put all dried fruit into the freezer for about 10
minutes. While you're waiting, process the nuts
into a coarse powder. Process 1 cup of chilled
dried fruit with the ground nuts. Transfer fruit-
nut mixture to a medium-sized bowl. Process
remaining dried fruit a cup at a time, with 2
tablespoons of carob powder for each cup of fruit.
Add honey and vanilla, if desired, to dried fruit
mixture and mix with a wooden spoon or your
hands. Press into a greased 6" cake pan. Place
pan in freezer for 10 minutes; run a table knife
around the inside rim and turn cake out onto a
flat plate or serving platter.

Hand-Crank Recycled Meat Grinder Method

If you've chosen this method, congratulations! It's quieter, gives you and your helpers some exercise, and uses no electricity. It also gives the cake a more consistent texture because it grinds the dried fruit more finely.

Put dried fruit into the carefully cleaned grinder and start cranking. After about half the fruit has been ground, add the nuts and finish with the rest of the fruit. When all fruit has been ground, check the consistency and taste to see if it needs any honey or rice syrup as binder, optional vanilla, or any carob powder to thicken the mixture, and add them accordingly.   Press into a greased 6" cake pan. Place pan in freezer for 10 minutes; run a table knife around the inside rim and turn cake out onto a flat plate or serving platter.

For a 9" layer, double the recipe; layer will be thinner than others because of the ratios involved. For a 12" layer, quadruple the recipe. We think this cake tastes best as a single layer with real cream cheese frosting.

Frosting

This is the only white frosting I could devise that didn't use refined sugar or dairy products. The soy cream cheese has casein, a milk protein, but this is as close to vegan as I could get. Most vegans would use the rice syrup instead of honey; this gives the frosting a slightly caramel flavor and a slightly darker color. The vanilla will additionally darken this frosting.

Make one recipe of this frosting to test-taste it; Soy Kaas frosting is not to everyone's taste. The amounts of honey or rice syrup are minimal; you may want to add more to suit your taste. If you don't like Soy Kaas, and aren't vegan, use a low-fat cream cheese such as Neufchatel instead. It's quite an improvement over the standard white grease-and-sugar frostings put on some bakery cakes.

To frost and fill the carrot cake recipe given above (3 tiers), make 12 cups of frosting. Give the Soy Kaas containers to an elementary teacher to use for art projects, or to someone who does a lot of crafts. This frosting pipes moderately well if the weather isn't too hot.

If you can't find it locally, try to order Soy Kaas through a local health food store or co-op. It is distributed by: American Natural Snacks, P.O. Box 1067, St. Augustine, FL 32085-1067.

"Cream Cheese" Frosting 1   about 1 cup

8 oz. Soy Kaas soy cream cheese
3 tablespoons honey or 4 tablespoons brown rice syrup
1 teaspoon vanilla, optional (alters color to off-white/ivory)

Beat all ingredients together until smooth. If not using immediately, store refrigerated in airtight container; otherwise frosting will have unattractive discolored edges like mayonnaise that has been left uncovered. Frost completely cooled cake at the last possible minute to avoid this same effect. As mentioned above, cream cheese or Neufchatel may be successfully substituted for the Soy Kaas.

"Cream Cheese" Frosting 2   about 1 1/4 cups

8 oz. Soy Kaas soy cream cheese
4 oz. soy margarine, softened at room
    temperature
3 tablespoons honey or 4 tablespoons brown
    rice syrup
1 teaspoon vanilla, optional (alters color to off-
    white/ivory)

Mix as for Cream Cheese Frosting 1 above. This breaks down in hot weather more easily than Frosting 1, and the margerine makes the color more ivory.

How to Tier a Cake

These instructions are for the Vegan Spice Wedding Cake, Vegan Carrot Spice Cake, and the Boiled Fruitcake. Traditionally, wedding cakes have three tiers, each two layers thick with frosting or filling in between—6", 9" and 12". This is supposed to feed 150 people. I recommend that you think more in terms of 75 to 85 people.

The detailed instructions below are much simpler than they seem, but I though it best to include all the details. Here are the steps to tiering a cake:

Equipment:
- The cake
- serving platter for the cake, at least 3" to 4" wider than the bottom 12" tier
- 1 length of 1/4" dowel (1 yard); next size larger or smaller is fine if you can't get 1/4"
- 9" cardboard round for bottom of 9" tier
- 6" cardboard round for bottom of 6" tier

1. Prepare and bake one recipe of Vegan Spice Wedding Cake, Vegan Carrot Spice Cake, or Boiled Fruitcake, dividing the batter into the prepared 6", 9" and 12" pans as described in the recipe. Pans should each be two thirds full; if you have to skimp on one, skimp on the 6" pan, since it will rise proportionately higher anyway.

2. Allow cake layers to cool for 10 minutes in the pan, and finish cooling right side up on cake racks.

3. While the layers are cooling, wash, dry and prepare the cake pans. Mix and bake a second batch of the same recipe; do everything the same as Steps 1 and 2.

4. While layers cool, prepare frosting. It is best to make the cake at least the day or evening before the wedding, prepare and refrigerate the frosting in an airtight container, and frost it just a few hours before the wedding.

5. Check all layers to make sure that the tops are level. If necessary, use a serrated knife to saw off any domed tops. Try to take off as little of the cake as you can; you want as much cake as possible, after all that work. For the first wedding cake I baked, I made the mistake of trying to use

frosting to fill in the gaps between the edges and the domed centers of each layer, instead of leveling the tops. Each tier tilted in a different direction. The cake was delicious, but it looked like a condemned skyscraper.

5. Let the frosting come to room temperature. With two large metal spatulas, lift and/or slide one of the 12" layers onto your chosen serving plate. The plate should be level, or the cake may buckle and split. Spread frosting or filling on that layer, and lift/slide/lower the other 12" layer onto its twin. Congratulations. You now have the bottom tier.

6. Frost the sides of the bottom tier, then the top. Now you're going to cut the doweling that will support the 9" tier. To find out how long to make the lengths, insert the dowel into the 12" tier until you hit bottom, marking the place with your thumb. Remove dowel, and saw that length off. Now saw five other pieces of doweling the same length. Insert the dowels into the cake within a 3 1/2" radius from the center.

7. Repeat step 5 for the 9" tier, putting the bottom layer onto the 9" cardboard round. Center the 9" tier onto the 12" tier.

8. Measure and cut 4 dowels to support the 6" tier. Insert the dowels into the 9" tier within a 2 1/2" radius from the center.

9. Repeat step 5 for the 6" tier, putting the bottom layer onto the 6" cardboard round. Center the 6" tier onto the 9" tier. Unless you have forgotten to frost the 6" tier, you are done!

Cake Decorations

Two ways to decorate your wedding cake without wasting resources are to use organically-grown edible flowers and piped frosting decorations. Of the two, edible flowers are my preference, because they don't require artificial coloring or manual dexterity. However, piped frosting decorations mean that you have nothing to grow or pick.

Piped Frosting Decorations

To pipe frosting for decorative effects, you can make a cone of parchment paper and cut the tip to make the icing flow out in certain patterns. An alternative is to make the cone and drop a decorating tip in the end. Environmentally speaking, a parchment paper cone is better than a plastic one, especially if you aren't going to be decorating dozens of cakes in the future.

IF YOU CARE™ Environment Friendly Products makes unbleached natural parchment paper for baking—and also in muffin cup form. IF YOU CARE™ is a product of Sweden. I've seen it in The Wooden Spoon catalog (1-800-431-2207; P.O. Box 931, Clinton, CT 06413-0931). It is imported by A.V. Olsson Trading Co. Inc., 10 Glenville St., Greenwich, CT 06831. When you finish piping the icing and have squeezed all the icing out, you can try composting your natural parchment paper cone, especially if you used tofu "cream cheese." For baking purposes, the paper is supposed to be nontoxic when incinerated.

Making a Parchment Pastry   Bag for Piped Frosting Decorations

If the parchment doesn't already come in triangular shapes, and is packaged in a roll, pull out enough paper to make a square, and cut it. Roll the parchment square into a cone.

Flatten the point of the cone

and cut it straight across to make a simple round "rope" of frosting.

The bigger the diameter of the hole, the larger the diameter of the frosting "rope."

To make leaves, cut a single notch in the paper tip.

To make stars, cut two notches.

To make roses, make a diagonal cut about 1/4" wide, and pinch one end so that the opening is an elongated teardrop shape. Make a tiny inverted cone of icing on the base of an inverted wine glass (instead of a "rose nail"), and squeeze icing out of tip while slowly rotating wine glass base to get a whorled rose of icing. Good luck.

Using a spoon, fill the parchment pastry bag about half full of frosting. Twist the top of the bag until there is no air space at the top. Squeeze the bag to expell air and a bit of frosting from the tip; otherwise your first piped decorations will break off or have air holes instead of a smooth surface.

For complete technical, illustrated instructions on piping all kinds of wonderful borders and artwork, and exactly what equipment to use for each, see *The Cake Bible*. It's a better investment than a cake decorating class, and if you decide that you don't want to make all those luscious cake and buttercream recipes, the book makes a terrific gift.

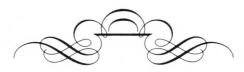

Edible Flowers

Edible flowers make nice cake decorations. A scattering of rose buds can hide a multitude of cake and icing flaws.

Good resources for information on edible flowers include Olga Essex' article in the summer 1994 issue of *Vegetarian Gourmet*; *Edible Flowers: From Garden to Palate* by Cathy Wilkinson Barash; and *The Complete Herb Book* by Maggie Stuckey.

From their writings and standard gardening books, I have devised the following list of edible flowers you may want to use to decorate the wedding cake, as garnishes, decorations, or even as components of the bouquets, corsages or boutonnieres. Do not eat any flower that has been sprayed, treated with chemicals of any kind, or has been growing near a road.

common name (species name)	color(s)
borage (Borago officinalis)	blue/purple
day lily (Hemerocallis)	ranges cream to burgundy
johnny-jump-up (Viola tricolor)	purple/ yellow/ white
nasturtium (Tropaeolum majus)	yellow, orange, red
pansy (Viola x Wittrockiana)	purples, blues, red, white, yellows
pinks, carnation (Dianthus caryophyllus)	ranges white to pink, magenta, red
scented geranium (Pelargonium graveolens, P. capitatum, P. crispum, P. denticulatum)	pink, violet
rose (Rosa)	virtually all colors

season	notes
spring to fall; varies with region	medicinally a diuretic; eat sparingly
summer	some bloom at night, wither in day
spring to summer	may be toxic in large quantities
summer to fall	medium-large flowers spicy taste
spring, fall	purple petals turn the eater's tongue purple
summer	spicy clove taste; petal base tastes bitter
summer	avoid eating the citronella scented geranium
summer	old-fashioned usually most fragrant, best tasting

Covering a cake with marzipan

If you're brave and have a knack for these sorts of things, a marzipan-covered cake may be just the sort of thing you want. The rest of us, however, will end up with a misshapen cake that looks like it has been covered in pale beige play-dough. Commercial marzipan such as Odense brand will probably yield the best results, if you're not bothered by the plastic tube packaging or the fact that it contains refined sugar. The recipes below are only for individuals who want an alternative to store-bought marzipan, are manually dexterous, and can work wonders with a blob of glorified nut butter.

Cashew Marzipan

This marzipan is delicious if you like raw cashews. Some people think it tastes like unadorned cashew butter, though. Try some to see whether you like it. It is definitely a pale beige color. For this recipe and the almond marzipan that follows, vegans can substitute brown rice syrup. Mix one cup at a time; it makes a great stuffing for pitted dates.

    1 cup raw cashew pieces
    2 tablespoons light-colored honey
    1 tablespoon safflower oil
    arrowroot powder for rolling out the marzipan

Process the cashew pieces and the honey. Add the safflower oil and process until smooth like nut butter. Sprinkle the work surface with arrowroot powder and turn the marzipan out onto it.

Knead until the marzipan is a smooth ball, adding arrowroot powder to the surface as necessary to prevent sticking. Roll out between 1/4"-1/8" thick. Run a long spatula under marzipan to ensure that it is not stuck to the work surface. With your hands and spatula, lift it onto the cake tier, taking care not to tear it. Good luck. Trim off excess marzipan from the bottom of the tier with a sharp knife, remove any cake crumbs, and knead it into the main batch for use in the next tier.

Make 9 cups to cover a 3-tier cake. Any extra can be used as stuffing for whole pitted dates.

Almond Marzipan

    2 cups almonds, blanched
    3 tablespoons light-colored honey
    1 tablespoon safflower oil

Use the same method as above. More traditional than the cashew marzipan.

Once all tiers of the cake are safely covered with marzipan, you can hide the "seams" or edges where the tiers meet in one of two ways:
• pipe a border with "cream cheese frosting;" or
• insert tiny, firm-stemmed edible flowers in the edges, with no spaces between the flowers. Poke a hole in the marzipan with a toothpick and insert the flower. Tiny rose buds would work well. This is decorative and hides the edges without adding any more fat and sugar to the cake.

Donating uneaten reception food to a shelter for the homeless

Many restaurants and caterers already do this as matter of regular practice—just ask if they do, or would be willing to do so. If it is not regular practice for them, get it written up in your catering contract, if necessary. If you aren't finding caterers who will donate leftover food, you may want to phone up a shelter and ask if they will give you names of caterers or restaurants that already donate to them—tell them you're looking for someone who will do this for your wedding reception. However, be understanding if they feel that they may be compromising the confidentiality of their donors by disclosing names.

Recycling

Be sure to recycle all bottles and cans. This is most easily done if you avoid beverages in plastic bottles, which do not recycle as easily as glass or aluminum. If you're not preparing the food yourselves, have the caterer include recycling of bottle and cans in your catering contract.

Finally...

Throughout this process, look for ways to obtain organic ingredients and purchase ingredients in bulk with your own containers. When you must buy something in packaging, look for materials that can be recycled or reused. In my area, Sucanat is not available in bulk. However, I can buy it in a two-kilo metal and cardboard container that makes a great drum or container for a child (or adult). Save up enough of them, and find a daycare, preschool or elementary teacher interested in using them for art projects, etc. Many items can be reused in this way. Simply refuse to buy items or packaging that must be thrown away.

Chapter 9: Odds and Ends— Candles, Favors, Cleanup, Departure

Wedding Favors

Traditionally, wedding guests are each given some small, tacky item that they will never use, or that will end up, at least in part, in a landfill. How many tiny plastic champagne glasses, tin wedding rings, or tufts of tulle stuffed with junk do we really need? Here are a few suggestions, some more labor-intensive than others. You can probably think of more.

• EnvirOmints—These fine chocolate mints with raised images of endangered animals are individually wrapped in foil, and have an enclosed picture/ information card about the animal and its endangered status. The company gives 50% of its profits to charitable wildlife causes. EnvirOnmintal Candy Co., Inc., P.O. Box 95730, Seattle, WA 98145; (206) 298-1230.

• Toucan Chocolates are gourmet chocolates made with nuts from the tropical rainforest. They are wrapped in attractive boxes made of 100% recycled paper. P.O. Box 72, Waban, MA 02168;

(617) 964-8696. See the Earth Care and Seventh Generation catalogs first.

• Those who enjoy labor-intensive activities can make their own chocolate wedding favors by melting fine quality tofu chocolate (see **An aside about chocolate** on the next page) and pouring it into molds. There are many different shapes available, not just the traditional wedding bells. In fact, avoid the wedding bell candy molds, which can only be used for weddings. Select a design that can be used on other occasions—stars, sea shells, flowers, abstract shapes. Choose shapes that are one solid piece and don't have a lot of fragile parts to break off or get stuck in the mold. Melt the chocolate over barely simmering water in the top of a double boiler. Do not get any water into the chocolate, or it will turn strange and grainy. Then pour the melted chocolate into the molds, which are usually come in a sheet of a dozen or so. Let cool at room temperature or in the refrigerator, then gently flex the sheet to loosen the chocolate shapes from the molds. Store in airtight container in a cool place until shortly before the wedding. You'll need to wrap the finished chocolates in something; I recommend folding an origami box of new, recycled-content paper for each guest's chocolate(s). The book *Origami Boxes* by Tomoko Fuse (New York: Japan Publications U.S.A., 1989) and recycled paper content origami paper have been available through Earth Care; see their catalog.

Once you've finished making your wedding favors, you can get extra mileage out of these molds by freezing juice or water in them to make novelty ice cubes for your punch bowl.

An aside about chocolate

Cloud Nine makes Tropical Source, a nondairy tofu chocolate that is quite nice. It is available in chocolate chip form (or in bars with pieces of dried fruit mixed in—good for eating, but the chips are best for cooking). They donate 10% of their profits "to assist local communities, tribes and organizations to produce ecologically sustainable tropical food products." Cloud Nine Inc., 720 Monroe St., Hoboken, NJ 07030; (201) 216-0382. Cloud Nine also makes organic chocolate that does not use lignin vanillin— apparently virtually every other chocolate manufacturer does. According to April Moore in *The Earth and You: Eating for Two,* in the manufacture of one pound of lignin-based vanillin, <u>over</u> <u>150</u> <u>pounds</u> of paper pulp mill waste are produced.

Another good company for chocolate is Rapunzel. They make organic Swiss chocolate, and have a special Eco-Trade program with the farmers who grow the ingredients. Rapunzel pays premium prices for the crops, so that the farmers can grow them organically instead of having to produce greater quantities to make a living wage. They use Madagascar Bourbon vanilla (not vanillin); whole cane sugar; and whole milk powder from free-range, organically-fed cows.

Rapunzel USA, 8060 Valencia Street, Aptos, CA 95003; 1-800-743-7840.

• desktop-published booklets—subjects could include your own poetry or prose, readings from the wedding ceremony, recipes, etc. You can make these yourselves very economically; just make sure they are something your guests will want to keep. Check around to find a printer who uses vegetable-based inks.

• Haiku on homemade recycled paper. Give each guest a haiku poem, handprinted on a piece of handmade recycled paper. This is nice, meaningful, inexpensive, and requires nothing disposable in the making or giving. Small Japanese maple leaves or pressed flowers can give the paper a very personal, distinctive look—experiment. Homemade recycled paper-making instructions are in Appendix A—Green Activities. You can even have a paper-making party well in advance of the wedding. Since haiku is generally nature oriented, it is ideally suited for a nature wedding theme.

Structurally, a haiku poem usually consists of three lines of five, seven, and five syllables respectively. It may describe a moment in nature or a natural scene. Haiku is unmetered and unrhymed.

Butterflies

In some parts of the country, couples are paying upwards of three hundred dollars to release hundreds of butterflies at the close of their ceremony. Environmentally, this doesn't seem like a good idea. Unless the butterflies are a species native to the area, you could be introducing a pest that could outcompete beneficial native insects and caterpillars, or overfeed on native vegetation. The destructive gypsy moth was introduced into this country by a man who thought he had found a substitute for silk worms.

Candles

For anything that requires a flame, be sure to have fire extinguishing materials readily available. Don't use candles or olive oil lamps out in the woods, unless you have a fire permit. It is your responsibility to use fire wisely, if at all. If in doubt, don't use it.

Paraffin is a petroleum product, and a nonrenewable resource. Beeswax is a renewable resource (although vegans may not choose to use it). Olive oil lamps are also another renewable resource lighting alternative. Beeswax candles are available in a wide variety of colors and forms, including solid tapers, not just the traditional rolled honeycomb texture most people associate with them. Before you look in catalogs, you might want to check in fine stationery and gift stores, food co-ops, or expanded health food stores. If the style or type that you want isn't available locally, here are some sources from catalogs:

Beeswax candles

• Busy Bee Candles has both honeycomb (in everything from votive to taper to pillar) and elegant solid taper styles in a wide range of colors and sizes. My favorites (available through gift shops here locally, but pictured in their brochure without an order number) are long, ivory 12" solid tapers spiraled with a helix-like shelf. They are simple but very elegant. At approximately $17.95 a pair, they're not for filling an entire candelabra, but they're the loveliest candles of any type I've seen yet. Phone 1-800-628-7965 between 8-4:30 Central Standard Time only; they are a family-run business.

• Check Earth Care, The Natural Choice and Seventh Generation catalogs.

Recycled-material candle holders

• Seventh Generation and Earth Care have had candle holders of recycled materials—glass and wrought iron fence finials. Check for what they may have in their latest catalogs.

Olive oil lamps

These are available in some gift shops, food co-ops, New Age bookstores, and catalogs. Used since biblical times, olive oil lamps are convenient for those of us who cook with olive oil; how often can cooking oil double as a light source in a power outage? Also, usually the wick is simply a twisted cotton string. (You can make your own replacement wicks with twisted-together leftover cotton strings from package string, bags of dry pet food, flour, etc.) Styles range from relatively inexpensive to more elegant and pricey.

• The least expensive lamp I found is a simple copper coil and wick (complete with instructions and how to make a new wick when the original is

used up) for $3.95, made by the Children's Kiva Project, Box 694, Drain, OR 97435. It needs a heatproof glass container, which could be a large votive container purchased from a thrift shop or garage sale. Done this way, these lamps could be used attractively and affordably as table decorations.
• See the Earth Care catalog.
• Elazar's Olive Oil Lamps (1-800-600-LAMP) have retail and wholesale catalogs available. Their lamps range in price from inexpensive on up, and use the cotton from the end of a cotton swab for the wick. (Perhaps thrifty recyclers among us can use the cotton from vitamin jars instead.) P.O. Box 1384, Longview, WA 98632-7815. Business hours 9 a.m.- 5 p.m. PST.

Guest book

Having a guest book for family and friends to sign at a wedding is a standard practice in most parts of the country. It can be useful to help you remember who was there, once the rush of the day is past. Use a blank book of recycled paper for your guest book. If you choose one with unlined paper, guests can write notes to you, or draw illustrations, which personalize the book. Try Langdell Paperworks (see description, address and phone number under Chapter 2—Invitations), and the Earth Care, The Natural Choice and Seventh Generation catalogs.

If you're really creative, bind your own handmade book for a guest book or photo album, using *The Art of the Handmade Book* by Flora Fennimore (Chicago Review Press, 1992). It's written for ages 10 and up, and makes a good gift for elementary teachers and young attendants.

Reception cleanup for do-it-yourselfers

• donate uneaten reception food to a local shelter for the homeless.

• Compost food (no meat, dairy, or vegetable oil, please!) and floral scraps.

• Recycle glass bottles, aluminum cans, steel cans, any paper or cardboard; and plastic, if you couldn't avoid using it.

• Use biodegradable, non-phosphate dish detergent for hand or automatic dishwashing.

• Use washable, reusable rags for wiping up spills; if you use paper towels, use recycled/unbleached/undyed.

• Choose trash bags made from recycled plastics (or recycled paper).

• Try club soda for stain removal on fabrics and upholstery.

• Read *Clean & Green: The Complete Guide to Nontoxic and Environmentally Safe House-keeping.* It has recipes for all kinds of homemade nontoxic cleaners, air fresheners, disinfectants, polishes, waxes, a thorough list of common stains and natural stain removers—virtually everything you need to know to eliminate toxins from your life and the environment.

Transportation

As mentioned earlier, you can save fuel and cut down on air pollution by holding your wedding and reception at the same location. A variation on this is to walk from the ceremony site to the reception site. Friends of ours had their wedding ceremony and reception at two different locations, with a post-wedding procession to the reception site. Bride, groom and guests walked about a quarter mile from their lakeside wedding site to their backyard reception, accompanied by strolling musicians.

If the majority of your guests are from out of town around the same area, you may want to save travel for them by having the wedding where the majority of your guests live. Encourage your guests to carpool to sites; perhaps have a friend or relative coordinate a carpool list, and contact guests. You could be responsible for introducing future lifelong friends, or even spouses !

The Departure

As you ride off into the sunset, skip the gas-guzzling limousine, and drive your economy car instead. There are horse-drawn carriages, but usually the horses have to be transported to and from the site in trailers, and the carriage ride can't be very long. But this doesn't mean that your leave-taking can't be distinctive. Friends of ours had what was probably the most fun—and unusual—departure from a conventional reception site ever. Dressed in their wedding duds, they rode away on a refurbished old tandem bicycle sporting a Just Married sign and dragging a couple of tin cans—the bride's floor-length dress tied up to avoid the spokes, the groom's tails flapping !

Chapter 10: Honeymoon

For a green honeymoon, consider cutting down on travel and choosing someplace nearby. This reduces the use of fossil fuels to get to your destination. It also cuts down on travel time and expense. Many couples admit to being so worn out by wedding preparations and travel to get to their honeymoon destination, that their wedding night was merely a long and much-needed sleep session. Because of this, I am an advocate of the local honeymoon. *Creative Weddings* authors Laurie Levin and Laura Golden Bellotti take this even one step further with The At-Home Honeymoon for those who can't get away. They have some good suggestions. After all, they say, it's a state of mind.

Green ways to make an inexpensive local honeymoon special:

• Don't overlook all the great places that are virtually in your back yard. Consider in advance what possibilities the area offers. There may be natural areas, historic landmarks, nightlife, etc. that you haven't explored yet—simply because they're next door. Get information on local attractions and lodgings through the Chamber of Commerce and local guidebooks.

• Assemble a fruit basket before you depart, then surprise your partner with it at your destination.

Select durable fruit in season and arrange attractively. Organically grown fruit is especially nice to bring. If the basket is small enough, you can fit it inside a grocery bag so he/she won't see it until you can sneak it into your room.
• Pack a simple vase and put some durable flowers in a cooler to arrange for your room.
• Bring a bottle of non-alcoholic sparkling cider and two champagne glasses.
• Buy a good book on massage from a second hand bookstore, and pack some massage oil.
• Pack some nice, biodegradable bubble bath. The Body Shop (see Personal Care section in Chapter 5) has nice bubble bath products.
• Float a few scented, nontoxic flowers on top of your bath water. Try roses or rose petals, jasmine, orange blossoms or lavendar.
• Bring a pair of beeswax candles and holders for a candlelit dinner if you're staying in a cabin or place with meal-preparing facilities.
• If you can find a good, recycled secondhand silk robe in a consignment shop, pack it.

Accommodations
Saunders Hotel Group, which includes the **Boston Park Plaza Hotel,** the **Lenox,** and **Copley Square,** has made the news several times as a green hotel group. According to an article by Shelby Siems in *The Christian Science Monitor* (May 20, 1994), the hotels' green practices include: installing water-conserving low-flow showerheads and low-flush toilets; recycling all their old phone books; using environmentally safe cleaning chemicals; installing bulk shampoo dis-

pensers instead of distributing hundreds of tiny plastic bottles; banning aerosols and Styrofoam; recycling bottles and cans; educating guests (bathroom plaques state, "It takes more than 2,000,000 gallons of clean water just to bathe and feed one adult for a year."); and contributing to an environmental fund. They range in size from quite grand (the Park Plaza) to intimate (Copley Square). The Park Plaza and the Lenox offer wedding packages; contact them or Copley Square for more information. Boston Park Plaza Hotel, main switchboard (617) 426-2000; weddings and catering (617) 457-2281. Lenox Hotel, main switchboard (617) 536-5300; Copley Square Hotel main switchboard (617) 536-9000.

Four Seasons Olympic, a 450-room luxury hotel in Seattle, has had its grand 1920s opulence restored, and is a registered National Historical Landmark. It recycles its pre-consumer food waste, cans and bottles, cardboard and paper—342 tons of it in 1994, according to Kirk Gormley in the May 1995 issue of *Enviro* ("Record Recycling Rate," pp. 16-17). They are a well-known venue for weddings and receptions, and the catering manager specializes in weddings. Phone the main switchboard at (206) 621-1700.

Green Suites International (GSI) is a small Los Angeles-based company that will convert selected standard hotel guest rooms into "Green Suites." To do this, they provide equipment for air filtration of individual rooms, recycled paper goods, nontoxic cleaning supplies, and all-natural toiletries (sometimes from refillable wall dispensers) to hotels. For a further investment, they will install nontoxic wall and floor coverings, organic cotton linens and towels, furniture made from sustainably-harvested lumber, and energy-efficient lighting. Most of their clients are in California, Arizona and Nevada, and include hotel rooms at: Holiday Inn, Radisson, Marriott, Piccadilly Inn, Doubletree, Ramada, ANA, and Bally's Las Vegas. Contact Green Suites International at 1-800-224-4228 or (310) 772-2892 for a list of their client hotels and the green amenities each offers.

Maho Bay Camps in Saint John, U.S. Virgin Islands, is a resort with tent cabins and villas, designed to be environmentally responsible. They use solar electricity and cistern-collected rain water, and recycled building materials and supplies: for example, foam insulation made of recycled milk jugs; and glass bathroom tiles of crushed recycled light bulbs. The tent-cabins are built up off the ground to preserve tortoise habitat. Contact 1-800-392-9004 or (212) 472-9453; or write Maho Bay Camps, 17A East 73rd St., New York, NY 10021.

Ecotourism
    Ecotourism is both a solution and a problem for the world's remaining natural areas. Generally defined as an educational vacation with an environmental focus, ecotourism generates real interest in endangered species and habitats, as

only personal experience can. However, it sometimes threatens the very areas it endeavors to save. Sometimes, indigenous people have been made to move from their homes—in order to accommodate a wildlife preserve, for example—with no viable options. The area's carrying capacity can be exceeded by too many outsiders coming through. Also, much of the money spent by ecotourists does not always stay in the local community. For example, in Nepal, less than 7% of the daily expenditures of trekkers stays in the villages the trekkers pass through, according to *Almanac of the Environment*. For a further discussion of ecotourism's advantages and disadvantages, see the article by Tensie Whelan in the National Audubon Society's *Almanac of the Environment*, and Chapter 4 of Daniel and Sally Grotta's *The Green Travel Sourcebook*.

If you are considering an ecotour-type honeymoon, keep the following points in mind. Effective ecotourism:

• funnels money back into the local economy—and the area being protected. It does the former by employing local people as tour guides, interpreters, managers, drivers, cooks, etc.; and by spending money at local accommodations and businesses. It does the latter by making donations above park or reserve fees, or perhaps by setting up a special trust fund for the areas patronized.
• uses local resources wisely, conforming to local standards of resource consumption. Although the United States has only 7% of the world's

population, its residents use one third of the world's resources. That needs to change.

• involves local people in the planning and administrative process. All too frequently in the past, a reserve would be set aside, and the indigenous people would be evicted and barred from using the resources they had previously used for food, shelter, and livelihood.

• takes carrying capacity of the site into consideration. Too many visitors, no matter how ecologically attuned, can spell disaster for a sensitive site.

• is respectful and responsible in its treatment of indigenous peoples, wildlife, and the environment.

Here are two examples of parks that have begun to work with the local population to preserve habitat and restore a way of life.

Richtersveld, a national park in South Africa, initiated a partnership between the national parks board and the local community in 1991. Fifty percent of the profits from tourism and a plant nursery returns to the community. The parks board leases community land for the park, and community members, employed by the board, run the park. According to an article by John Battersby in *The Christian Science Monitor* (August 23, 1994), this is the first time in which an indigenous community was actively involved in running a park. It has served as a model for Riemvasmaak.

Also mentioned in Battersby's article is Riemvasmaak, another South African national park. In February 1994 Riemvasmaak restored legal rights to former residents to reoccupy 172,000 acres from which they were forcibly removed in 1973 and 1974. Community members had been evicted from their homes so that the park could be expanded. Now a nearby community will be offered a monthly rental for the part of their land occupied by the park, and there is the possibility of about 70 jobs for community members.

For further information on either of these parks, contact the South African Tourism Board, 500 5th Ave 20th Floor, New York, NY 10110; telephone (212) 730-2929.
Or: South African Tourist Board, 9841 Airport Boulevard, Suite 1524, Los Angeles, CA 90045; telephone (310) 641-8444.

For a list of ecotourism outfits, see the following resources:

• *EcoTraveler* magazine. Skies of America Publishing Co., 7730 S.W. Mohawk Street, Tualatin, OR 97062; (503) 691-1955. Established 1979. Articles about current trips offered. Tips for travelers and a directory of "eco and adventure" tour operators.
• Foehr, Stephen. *Eco-Journeys: The World Guide to Ecologically Aware Travel and Adventure.* Chicago: The Noble Press, Inc., 1993. Categorizes trips according to the type of experience it will be—"Safe Thrills," Family,"

"Raw Adventure," "Special Needs," etc., and then by region within each category. For each trip, it lists specific tour operators, with names, addresses and phone numbers at the back of the book.

• Geffen, Alice M. and Berglie, Carole. *Eco Tours and Nature Getaways: A Guide to Environmental Vacations Around the World.* New York: Clarkson Potter/ Publishers, 1993. Details tour operators and their trips. Organized by region or country, with geographical and trip indices at the back of the book. Good travel advice.

• Grotta, Daniel, and Sally Wiener Grotta. *The Green Travel Sourcebook: A Guide for the Physically Active, the Intellectually Curious, or the Socially Aware.* New York: John Wiley & Sons, Inc., 1992. A very thorough resource that includes tips for the eco-traveler, comments on the various tour groups and what they do for the local economy/environment, and information on trips. My favorite.

• Holing, Dwight. *A Guide to Earthtrips: Nature Travel on a Fragile Planet.* Venice, California: Living Planet Press, 1991. Describes the natural features (including parks and preserves) of seven major regions of the world. Includes a list of tour operators and travel agencies, nature-study travel programs, and a section on volunteer vacations.

• Kaye, Evelyn. *Eco Vacations: Enjoy Yourself and Save the Earth.* Leonia, New Jersey: Blue Penguin Publications, 1991. Publisher's address: Blue Penguin Publications, 147 Sylvan Ave., Leonia, NJ 07605. Following several lists that categorize tour organizations by destination, type of tour, and recommended age ranges for participants, each organization is briefly described, with address for further information. Includes the Audubon Ecotourism ethics code. An introductory book to get you started.

• Makower, Joel, with John Elkington and Julia Hailes. *The Green Consumer.* Rev. ed. (New York: Penguin Books, 1988). Don't buy this book for the tour operator listings alone, but if you already have a copy, it can be a good resource—especially the tips for what to find out about a tour operator beforehand.

• *National Green Pages,* Co-op America, 1612 K St. NW, #600, Washington, DC 20006; phone (202) 872-5307. Businesses in this directory have made a commitment to green practices. Look in their "Travel" section for up-to-date listings of ecotour operators and other green travel opportunities.

• Tovey, Priscilla. *Smart Vacations: the Traveler's Guide to Learning Adventures Abroad.* New York: St. Martin's Press, 1993. Lists and describes organizations offering educational vacations from archaeological digs or art history to the Zoological Society of Philadelphia's wildlife workshops.

Resources:

Selected Bibliography

Books

Baldwin, J., ed. *Whole Earth Ecolog.* New York: Harmony Books, 1990.

Barash, Cathy Wilkinson. *Edible Flowers: From Garden to Palate.* Golden, Colorado: Fulcrum Publishing, 1993.

Beranbaum, Rose Levy. *The Cake Bible.* New York: William Morrow and Company, Inc., 1988.

Berthold-Bond, Annie. *Clean & Green: The Complete Guide to Nontoxic and Environmentally Safe Housekeeping.* Woodstock, New York: Ceres Press, 1990.

Brown, Gail. *Sensational Silk.* Portland, Oregon: Palmer-Pletsch Associates, 1982.

Brown, Gail, and Karen Dillon. *Sew a Beautiful Wedding.* Portland, Oregon: Palmer-Pletsch Associates, 1980.

Butler, C. T. Lawrence, and Keith McHenry. *Food Not Bombs.* Philadelphia: New Society Publishers, 1992.

Cailliet, Greg, Paulette Setzer, and Milton Love. *Everyman's Guide to Ecological Living.* New York: The MacMillan Company, 1971.

Clark, David E. *Sunset New Western Garden Book.* Menlo Park, California: Lane Publishing Co., 1979.

Clifton, Claire. *Edible Flowers.* New York: McGraw-Hill Book Company, 1983.

Cole, Harriette. *Jumping the Broom: the African-American Wedding Planner.* New York: Henry Holt & Co., 1992.

Co-op America. *National Green Pages.* Co-op America, 1612 K Street NW, Suite 600, Washington, DC 20077-2573; 1-800-584-7336.

Dacyzyn, Amy. *The Tightwad Gazette.* New York: Villard Books, 1993.

Dadd, Debra Lynn. *Nontoxic, Natural & Earthwise.* New York: The Putnam Publishing Group, 1990.

Dadd-Redalia, Debra. *Sustaining The Earth: Choosing Products that are Safe for You, Your Family, and the Earth.* New York: Hearst Books, 1994.

Diamant, Anita. *The New Jewish Wedding.* New York: Summit Books, 1985.

The Earthworks Group. *50 Simple Things You Can Do to Save the Earth.* Berkeley, CA: Earthworks Press, 1989.

Elgin, Duane. *Voluntary Simplicity.* rev. ed. New York: William Morrow, 1993.

The Evergreen Alliance. *The New Green Christmas.* Mill Valley, California: Halo Books, 1991. (Address: Halo Books, 168 Morning Sun Avenue, Mill Valley, CA 94941; (415) 388-7206).

Farmer, Fannie Merritt. *The Fannie Farmer Cookbook.* 12th ed. New York: Bantam Books, 1983.

Findlater, Evelyn. *The Natural Entertainer.* London: Century Hutchinson Ltd., 1987.

Foehr, Stephen. *Eco-Journeys: The World Guide to Ecologically Aware Travel and Adventure.* Chicago: The Noble Press, Inc., 1993.

Geffen, Alice M. and Carole Berglie. *Eco Tours and Nature Getaways: A Guide to Environmental Vacations Around the World.* New York: Clarkson Potter Publishers, 1993.

Geiskopf-Hadler, Susann, and Mindy Toomay. *The Vegan Gourmet.* Rocklin, California: Prima Publishing, 1995. (Address: Prima Publishing, P.O. Box 1260, Rocklin, CA 95677; (916) 632-4400).

Goldbeck, Nikki and David. *Choose to Reuse.* Woodstock, New York: Ceres Press, 1995.

Grotta, Daniel, and Sally Wiener Grotta. *The Green Travel Sourcebook: A Guide for the Physically Active, the Intellectually Curious, or the Socially Aware.* New York: John Wiley & Sons, Inc., 1992.

Guren, Denise, and Nealy Gillete. *The Ovulation Method: Cycles of Fertility.* Can be ordered through Denise Guren, 2908 Cottonwood, Bellingham, WA 98225. (360) 733-2044.

Hacker, Randi. *How to Live Green, Cheap, and Happy: Save Money! Save the Planet!* Mechanicsburg, Pennsylvania: Stackpole Books, 1994.

Harms, Valerie. *The National Audubon Society's Almanac of the Environment.* New York: G. P. Putnam, 1994.

Hay, Roy, and Patrick M. Synge. *The Color Dictionary of Flowers and Plants.* New York: Crown Publishers, Inc., 1969.

Hillier, Malcolm. *The Book of Fresh Flowers: A Complete Guide to Selecting & Arranging.* New York: Simon and Schuster, 1988.

Holing, Dwight. *A Guide to Earthtrips: Nature Travel on a Fragile Planet..* Venice, California: Living Planet Press, 1991.

Hollister, Benjamin, Rosalyn Will, and Alice Tepper Marlin. *Shopping for a Better World.* San Francisco: Sierra Club Books, 1994.

Imber Black, Evan, Ph.D., and Janine Roberts, Ed.D. *Rituals for Our Times.* New York: Harper Collins, 1992.

Kaye, Evelyn. *Eco Vacations: Enjoy Yourself and Save the Earth.* Leonia, New Jersey: Blue Penguin Publications, 1991. Publisher's address: Blue Penguin Publications, 147 Sylvan Ave., Leonia, NJ 07605.

Kirschenbaum, Howard, and Rockwell Stensrud. *The Wedding Book.* New York: The Seabury Press, 1974.

Lappé, Marc. *Chemical Deception: the Toxic Threat to Health and Environment.* San Francisco: Sierra Club Books, 1991.

Levin, Laurie, and Laura Golden Bellotti. *Creative Weddings.* New York: Penguin, 1994.

Leviton, Richard. *Weddings By Design.* San Francisco: Harper San Francisco, 1993.

MacEachern, Diane. *Save Our Planet: 750 Everyday Ways You Can Help Clean Up the Earth.* New York: Dell Publishing, 1990.

Makower, Joel, with John Elkington and Julia Hailes. *The Green Consumer*. Rev. ed. New York: Penguin Books, 1988.

Metrick, Syndey Barbara. *I Do—A Guide to Creating Your Own Unique Wedding Ceremony*. Berkeley, California: Celestial Arts, 1992.

Moore, April. *The Earth and You: Eating for Two*. Washington, D.C.: Potomac Valley Press, 1993.

Mullins, Russ. *Report on internship with Northwest Air Pollution Authority*. Bellingham, Washington: Huxley College of Environmental Studies, Western Washington University, 1981.

Naylor, Sharon. *1001 Ways to Save Money...and Still Have a Dazzling Wedding*. Chicago: Contemporary Books, 1994.

Packer, Jane. *Flowers for All Seasons*. New York: Fawcett Columbine, 1989. (This is a series of four books, one for each season. Each has seasonal wedding flower ideas.)

Packham, Jo. *Wedding Flowers: Choosing and Making Beautiful Bouquets & Arrangements*. New York: Sterling Publishing Company, Inc., 1993.

Post, Elizabeth L. *Emily Post's Etiquette*. 14th ed. New York: Harper Collins, 1984.

Roberts, Elizabeth, and Elias Amidon, eds. *Earth Prayers*. San Francisco: Harper San Francisco, 1991.

Robertson, Laurel, Carol Flinders, and Brian Ruppenthal. *The New Laurel's Kitchen*. Berkeley, California: Ten Speed Press, 1986.

Rogers, Barbara Radcliffe. *The Encyclopedia of Everlastings: The Complete Guide to Growing, Preserving, and Arranging Dried Flowers*. New York: Weidenfeld & Nicholson, 1988.

Rogers, Jennifer. *Tried and Trousseau*. New York: Fireside Books (imprint of Simon & Schuster), 1992.

Samuels, Mike, M.D., and Hal Zina Bennett. *Well Body, Well Earth*. San Francisco: Sierra Club Books, 1983.

Sass, Lorna J. *Recipes from an Ecological Kitchen*. New York: William Morrow and Company, Inc., 1992.

Stoner, Carroll. *Weddings for Grownups.* San Francisco: Chronicle Books, 1993.

Stuckey, Maggie. *The Complete Herb Book.* New York: Berkeley Books, 1994.

Sunset New Western Garden Book. Menlo Park, California: Lane Publishing Company, 1979.

Teitel, Martin. *Rain Forest in Your Kitchen.* Washington, D.C./Covelo, California: Island Press, 1992.

Tovey, Priscilla. *Smart Vacations: the Traveler's Guide to Learning Adventures Abroad.* New York: St. Martin's Press, 1993.

Van Matre, Steve, and Bill Weiler, eds. *The Earth Speaks.* Warrenville, Illinois: The Institute for Earth Education, 1983.

Wasik, John F. *The Green Supermarket Shopping Guide.* New York: Warner Books, Inc., 1993.

Williams, Dar. *The Tofu Tollbooth.* Northampton, Massachusetts: Ardwork Press, 1994. Address: Ardwork Press, P. O Box 814, Northampton, MA 01061-0814.

Wilson, Jim. *Landscaping With Wildflowers: An Environmental Approach to Gardening.* Boston: Houghton Mifflin Company, 1992.

Winter, Ruth. *A Consumer's Dictionary of Household, Yard and Office Chemicals.* New York: Crown Publishers, Inc., 1992.

Articles

Battersby, John. "A Human Face for South Africa's Park System." *The Christian Science Monitor.* August 23, 1994. pp. 12-13.

Essex, Olga. "Waiter, There's a Flower Garden on My Plate!" *Vegetarian Gourmet.* No. 10. Vol. 3, issue 2 (Summer 1994), pp. 34-38, 59.

Ganis, Richard. "Toward a Good Hair Day." *E Magazine.* (July/August 1993), p. 12.

Gillette, Becky. "Indoor Pollution Solution." *Practical Homeowner.* Vol. II, no. 7 (Sept., 1987), pp. 18, 95.

Gormley, Kirk. "Record Recycling Rate." *Enviro.* Vol. 2, No. 4 (May 1995), pp. 16-17.

Kayte, Lillian. "A Wedding Day Buffet." *Veggie Life.* Vol. 1, No. 2 (July 1993), pp. 14-23.

Nixon, Will. "E Notes—The Bride Wore Green."*E Magazine.* Vol. III, No. 6. (November/ December 1992), p. 44.

O'Neil, Kelly. "Designer Fountain Pens Make Their Point." *The Christian Science Monitor* (March 28, 1994).

Robson, Mary. "It's not too late..." (bulb forcing). *The Seattle Times.* Sunday, December 12, 1993, pp. E1-2.

Spaid, Elizabeth Levitan. "Taking a Vow to Make Tasty Wedding Cakes." *The Christian Science Monitor* (June 23, 1994).

Tompor, Susan. "Saying 'I do' to cutting costs." *The Bellingham Herald.* Saturday, April 8, 1995, p. A7.

Wahl, Linda M. (Keener). "An Old-Fashioned Gown." *Sew Beautiful.* Vol. 7, no. 2 (issue #32; Special Occasions 1993), pp. 94-95.

Magazines

Audubon, The Magazine of the National Audubon Society, National Audubon Society, 950 3rd Avenue, New York, NY 10022-2705. Nature-oriented.

EcoTraveler. Skies of America Publishing Co., 7730 S.W. Mohawk Street, Tualatin, OR 97062; (503) 691-1955.

E Magazine., P.O. Box 5098, Westport, CT 06881; (203) 854-5559.

ENVIRO. P.O. Box 39420, Tacoma, WA 98439-0420; (206) 475-4346. A business magazine; member of Wasington Environmental Industry Association, Association of Washington Business, and Environmental Marketing Association.

IN BUSINESS, 419 State Ave., Emmaus, PA 18049. Bimonthly magazine detailing green businesses and trends.

Although generally not a consumer magazine, this is a good source for finding out about green products and services you might not otherwise hear about. (It's where I read about Green Suites International—see Chapter 10).

Newsletters

Many times newsletters can give you up-to-the-minute information that magazines with their distant deadlines cannot print until several months later. Each of the newsletters mentioned here is produced by the author of one of the books listed in the bibliography; the book title and author follow the newsletter information.

Conscious Consumer Newsletter, New Consumer Institute, P.O. Box 51, Wauconda, IL 60084. *The Green Supermarket Shopping Guide*, John F. Wasik. Information on environmentally sound products and practices.

The Green Consumer Letter, 1526 Connecticut Ave. NW, Washington, D.C. 20036; 1-800-955-GREEN or 202-332-1700. Edited by Joel Makower, author of *The Green Consumer*. Green lifestyle, and information on environmentally sound products.

Green-keeping, Box 110, Annandale, NY 12504. *Clean & Green*, Annie Berthold-Bond. Practical information on nontoxic and environmentally safe alternatives to various chemicals and substances used in everyday living.

Green Weddings, P. O. Box 29292, Bellingham, WA 98228-1292. A quarterly newletter to keep the information in this book up-to-date.

The Tightwad Gazette, RR1 Box 3570, Leeds, ME 04263. Practical information on how to live—and enjoy—a frugal, less-is-more lifestyle. A collection of a year's worth of these newsletters comprise the book, *The Tightwad Gazette*, by Amy Dacyczyn.

Catalogs

Note: Only request catalogs from companies whose products genuinely interest you. Share your catalogs with interested friends, and recycle the catalogs once they are out of date. For additional companies with catalogs, see the *National Green Pages* or *The Green Consumer*.

The Body Shop, 45 Horsehill Road, Cedar Knolls, NJ 07927; phone 1-800-541-2535. Personal care products for hair and skin. Environmentally responsible, and no animal testing.

Earth Care, Ukiah, CA 95482-3471; phone 1-800-347-0070. Earth-friendly personal, household and gift items.

Garden Botanika, 8624 154th Avenue N.E., Redmond, WA 98052; phone 1-800-877-9603. Natural cosmetics and body care products with botanical ingredients and minimal packaging.

Garnet Hill, 262 Main Street, Franconia, NH 03580; 1-800-622-6216. Natural fiber clothing, bedding and linens, lingerie and tights. Some green and organic cotton products.

The Natural Choice, Eco Design Co. 1365 Rufina Circle, Santa Fe, New Mexico 87501. (505) 438-3448. Organic cotton clothing, cosmetics, paints, household supplies.

The Ohio Hempery, Inc., 7002 State Route 329, Guysville, OH 45735; phone 1-800-BUY HEMP (that's 1-800-289-4367) or (614) 662-4367. Source of hemp and hemp blend fabrics.

Real Goods, 966 Mazzoni Street, Ukiah, CA 95482-3471; phone 1-800-762-7325.

Seventh Generation, 49 Hercules Drive, Colchester, VT 05446-1672; phone 1-800-456-1177.

Whole Earth Ecolog, Whole Earth Access, 2990 Seventh Street, Berkeley, CA 94710; 1-800-845-2000; (415) 845-3000.

Appendix

Recycled Papermaking

Equipment: mixed scrap paper, dishpan or tub, water, kitchen blender, old towels, framed screen smaller than dimensions of the dishpan, old empty frame smaller than the screen (will be the dimensions of the finished paper; 5" x 7" is a nice size), sponge, newspaper or cardboard, old dryer fabric softener sheets, cheesecloth or other lightweight, nonstick fabrics. Instead of a picture frame, you can use a large, open cookie cutter for unique shapes such as a heart, tree, etc.

Fill the blender with water. Tear up two 8 1/2 x 11 inch sheets of scrap paper into pieces the size of postage stamps. Add a handful to the blender and blend until cloudy, about 20 seconds. Put this in the tub and add water until tub is half full; the resultant mixture is called slurry. Blend the rest of the scraps with water and add to mixture in tub. The thicker the slurry, the thicker the paper will be, and vice versa. Place the empty frame on top of the screen, and hold securely with your hands. Have someone stir up the slurry so that all the paper fibers do not sink to the bottom of the tub. Dip the screen and frame down into the slurry with a scooping motion, and quickly lift it out of the tub, keeping it level. Hold it over the tub to allow water to drain. Brush away excess paper fibers outside the empty frame, and return them to the slurry. Remove the frame, lifting straight up, and you should have a fairly decent square of homemade paper. Place a newspaper section or piece of cardboard on it, and flip the whole unit over together—frame, new paper, cardboard. Leave the screen in place. Blot paper with the sponge, pressing each area once and wringing it out. Lift screen off of paper, tapping it gently if it sticks.

If desired, you can add confetti, glitter, dried flowers or small leaves at this stage. Place them exactly where you want them on the paper, and pour a minuscule amount of slurry on them to cement in place. Japanese maple leaves look nice, especially if the slurry has tiny twigs and bits of leaf. Cover the paper with a fabric softener sheet and continue to sponge water out of the paper until it is as dry as possible. Paper can either be air-dried or ironed dry between discarded fabric softener sheets, clean old cheesecloth, etc.

If you're making your own invitations, keep in mind that the smallest size of postcard or envelope the post office will take is 3 1/2" x 5."

Cornstarch Clay   makes a 4"-5" blob

2 cups baking soda
1 cup cornstarch
1 cup cold water

Combine baking soda and cornstarch in a saucepan. Add water slowly, stirring with a spoon that will not bend or break, preferably a thick-handled wooden one. Cook over low heat for 5-7 minutes, or until mixture is the consistency of mashed potatoes. Turn out onto a clean, heatproof surface to cool, and cover with a damp cloth to keep clay from drying out. When cool, knead for several minutes until pliable. This clay is most pliable at room temperature. If you have tender-stemmed flowers, use freshly-made, unrefrigerated cornstarch clay. If you have woody-stemmed, heavy flowers, form fresh clay into the shape you want it to be for the wedding flower arrangement, and store it airtight in the refrigerator until needed. Once refrigerated, the clay is much tougher, more like moderately brittle modeling clay. When this clay's duty as a floral support is done, pick out any stray leaves or petals and give it to a child to use as modeling clay. This is assuming that you have used edible, nontoxic flowers. This clay eventually will turn moldy if not made into shapes and dried; lengthen its life by refrigerating in an airtight container it when not in use. Shapes made with it may be air dried in 24 hours, or baked at 200 degrees F for two hours or so.

If it becomes dried out, this clay can be rejuvenated by soaking it in water almost to cover 20 minutes, then draining half of water, breaking clay into pieces and letting it absorb rest of water. Continue draining and breaking into smaller and smaller pieces until all the water is absorbed and all the tiny lumps are broken up. The clay will still be fairly elastic, but you may find it hard to break up all the very tiniest lumps if you want the original fine texture. Compost clay if it becomes moldy. It has a high salt content because of the baking soda, but should be fairly harmless if only one batch is composted at a time; break it into small pieces.

Because of the high salt content of this clay, it does not make a good preservative for live flowers.

Index

almond marzipan 127
Appendix 156-157
      cornstarch clay 156-157
      homemade recycled paper 156
articles 152-153
balloons, detrimental effect of 67
bibliography 148-155
Boston Park Plaza hotel 140-141
bridal shower activities—see recycled paper, homemade
bulk foods 93
butterflies, reasons not to release at weddings 133-134
cake decorating 120-128
cake recipes 107-115
      boiled fruitcake 111
      carob fruitcake 114-115
      matrimonial cake 112-113
      vegan carrot spice cake 110-111
      vegan spice cake 109
cake tops 105; see also cake decorating
candles 134-135
cashew marzipan 126
catalogs 155
chocolate 130-133
      Cloud Nine 132
      Envir-O-mints 130
      Rapunzel 132-133
      Toucan Chocolates 130-131
      waste from chocolate manufacture 130
contraception 63-64
Co-op America 8, 148
Copley Square 140-141
cornstarch clay 156-157
cosmetics, natural 57

deodorant 56
dry cleaning 40
ecotourism 142-147
edible flowers 123-125
everlastings (dried flowers) 81-84
fabric, organically-grown natural fiber 45-48
flowers 68-84
        corsages and boutonnieres, alternatives 72-73
        dried 81-84
        edible 123-125
        in a basket 74
        nosegay 73
        organically grown 69, 77-80
        presentation bouquet 75-76
food co-ops 95
fountain pens 27
frosting recipes 115-117
        almond marzipan 127
        cashew marzipan 126
        "cream cheese" frosting 115-117
gifts 87-92
        charitable donations in lieu of 91-92
        green 87, 88-91
glass pens 27-28
green hotels 140-142
        Boston Park Plaza 140-141
        Copley Square 140-141
        Four Seasons Olympic 141
        The Lenox 140-141
Green Suites International 141-142
green wedding 8-14
        definition 8-11
        general principles 12-14
Green Weddings newsletter 7, 154, 164
guest book 29, 136
hair care 57-60
handkerchiefs 52
hats 42, 49
honeymoon 139-147
invitations 26-32
jewelry cleaner 51
Lenox Hotel, the 140-141
lip salve or moisturizer recipe 56

Maho Bay Camps 142
menstrual pads, nondisposable 61-63
music, musicians 85-86
National Green Pages   8, 95, 148
natural fibers   45-48
      cotton 46-47
      organically grown 45-46
      silk 42, 64
natural fiber wedding clothes, ready-made 48-49
nature readings, sources of 38-39
nonalcoholic reception, advantages of 9-10
nosegays 73
olive oil lamps 135-136
organic ingredients, importance of 94-95
Origami Boxes   131
pens 27-28
      fountain 27
      glass 27-28
photo albums 29, 86-87, 136
photography 86
planning checklist 18-19
planning timeline 20-25
posy holders 72-73
presentation bouquet 75-76
punch recipe 102
rag curls 58-59
reception 33-36
      advantage of same location as wedding 33
      in fragile wilderness 34-36
      outdoor 34-36
reception locations 33-36
recipes:
      cakes 107-115
      duxelles 98-99
      "cream cheese" frosting
      marzipan 126-127
      punch 102
recycled paper, homemade 156
rented greenery 67
response cards 31-32
Richtersveld 144
Riemvasmaak 145
rings 50-51

shaving:
>> alternatives to aerosol shaving cream 55-56
>> alternatives to disposable razors 55
shoes 49-50
spray starch, safe homemade 76
stamps 26
streamers, recycled paper 67-68
tagua nuts 46, 51-52
toothpaste, baking soda and cloves 55
transportation 137-138
vegetarian reception recipes:
>> béchamel (white) sauce 100
>> duxelles 98-99
>> other sources:
>>> *Food Not Bombs* 97, 148 (Butler)
>>> *The Natural Entertainer* 96-97, 149 (Findlater)
>>> *The Vegan Gourmet* 95-96, 149 (Geiskopf-Hadler)
>>> *Veggie Life Magazine* 153 (Kayte)
>> wedding cakes 108-114
vintage clothing patterns 46-48, 64-66
water conservation 53-54
wedding cake recipes—see cake recipes
wedding clothes 40-52
>> attendants' 44-45
>>> women's 41-43, 52
>>> men's 43-44, 52
>>> children's 45
>> bride's 41-43, 45-50, 52
>> groom's 43-44, 45-50, 52
>> natural fiber 45-50
>> washable 41-42, 44
wedding favors:
>> chocolates 130-133
>> desktop-published books 133
>> haiku on homemade recycled paper 133
>> pitted dates stuffed with cashew marzipan 126
work party, pre-wedding 20, 23
wines, organic 101
winter flowers, forced 77-80

About the author

Carol Reed-Jones is a writer and music teacher living and working in the Pacific Northwest. She has a Master's degree in Music History. Her first children's book, *The Tree in the Ancient Forest*, was published in 1995 by DAWN Publications.

Carol is the editor of the quarterly *Green Weddings Newsletter*, which has current information on products and services of interest to those planning a wedding. It is available through Paper Crane Press, P. O. Box 29292, Bellingham, WA 98228-1292; (360) 676-0266.

To order more copies of this book, contact

Paper Crane Press
P. O. Box 29292
Bellingham, WA 98228-1292

phone: (360) 676-0266

We welcome your comments about *Green Weddings,* and your suggestions for future editions.

Notes

Notes

Notes

Notes

Notes

Notes

Notes

Notes

Notes